Renewing
America's Schools

Carl D. Glickman

Renewing America's Schools

A GUIDE FOR SCHOOL-BASED ACTION

Jossey-Bass Publishers · San Francisco

FIRST PAPERBACK EDITION PUBLISHED IN 1998.

Substantial discounts on bulk quantities of Jossey-Bass books are available to corporations, professional associations, and other organizations. For details and discount information, contact the special sales department at Jossey-Bass Inc., Publishers.
(415) 433-1740; Fax (800) 605-2665.

Manufactured in the United States of America on Lyons Falls Turin Book. This paper is acid-free and 100 percent totally chlorine-free.

For sales outside the United States, please contact your local Simon & Schuster International Office.

Jossey-Bass Web address: http://www.josseybass.com

Library of Congress Cataloging-in-Publication Data

Glickman, Carl D.
    Renewing America's schools : a guide for school-based action /
Carl D. Glickman. – 1st ed.
        p.   cm. – (The Jossey-Bass education series)
    Includes bibliographical references (p.   ) and index.
    ISBN 1-55542-543-7 (alk. paper)
    ISBN 0-7879-4065-8 (paperback)
    1. School improvement programs – United States.   2. Educational change – United States.   I. Title.   II. Series.
LB2822.82.G57   1993
    371.200973 – dc20   92-42860

FIRST EDITION
HB Printing   10 9 8 7
PB Printing   10 9 8 7 6 5 4 3 2 1

THE JOSSEY-BASS
EDUCATION SERIES

Contents

Preface

I accepted the assignment to write this book because of all the committed educators and citizens who have asked me the most basic of questions: How does one go about improving the education of students in public schools? Responding to that question has been the passion of my professional and personal life.

I have served on educational policy commissions, I have studied school change, and I have been a consultant to many individual schools, districts, states, and provinces in North America. Nevertheless, I believe that the reason this question has been posed to me so often is the up-close work in which I have been engaged over the past twenty-five years — from being a school principal in New England to being the director and orchestrator of a school renewal collaboration with more than sixty elementary, middle, and secondary schools in the state of Georgia. My most recent work has been assisting other agencies (districts, regional service agencies, and state departments) to set up similar collaborations with public schools, focused on educational renewal.

Over the years, I have come to the realization that the answer to that most basic question always has been right before our eyes. The answer is simple. The implementation is difficult, but it is the only hope for our public school students and for our institutions of public education. The answer is threefold:

1. We must realize that the basic goal of our schools is to prepare students to engage productively in a democracy.
2. We must organize and operate our own schools in accord with the democratic principles of our society.
3. Teaching and learning between students and teachers must demonstrate, in actions, the relationship between education and democracy—the power of learning for engagement in real issues.

Thus the answer right before us is democracy.

Stating the obvious is of little help, of course, and knowing what the answer is provides little guidance for making it a reality. My challenge has been to lay out clearly the premises and practices of how schools become democratic, moral, and purposeful. Basic questions and simple answers lead to profound changes in the conceptualization and operation of our nation's schools. In this book, I have tried to avoid educational jargon. I have taken a bludgeon to the "hot" educational fads and innovations of today and yesterday, and I am sure that this book will offend many well-intentioned reformers. I am sorry for such offenses, but the work of public education is too vital to the fulfillment of our democracy's enduring principles for me to be anything less than straightforward and honest.

Overview of the Contents

Chapter One introduces the need for schools to reclarify their enduring purpose in a democratic society and provides an overview of the status of public education as quite different from most commission reports and media stories. In Part One, I elaborate on the necessary three-dimensional framework for a moral and democratic school. Chapter Two explores the first dimension, that of developing a school covenant guided by core values of education in a democracy and by principles of teaching and learning. Chapter Three explains the second dimension, which entails developing a charter for school decision making that activates the covenant. Chapter Four describes the final dimension, the critical-study process that assists a school in making informed decisions and assessing student learning.

Part Two outlines the internal educational work of schools as well as the policy changes needed in districts and states, and concludes with the need to view school renewal as an ongoing process. Chapter Five describes the educational tasks (curriculum, staff development, coaching, instructional programs, staffing, time, and budgets) that schools have within their control. Chapter Six focuses on the internal issues that a school community must anticipate and resolve to give more confidence to its efforts. Chapter Seven raises provocative questions about comparing current educational practices with optimal conditions of learning. Chapter Eight describes the critical role, responsibilities, and policies needed of districts, school boards, and teacher associations/unions to clarify, encourage, coordinate, and support school renewal. Chapter Nine anticipates the various dilemmas and competing consequences of profound school change in reference to resistance, miscommunication, and dysfunctional behavior. Chapter Ten concludes with a realistic portrayal of what school communities can achieve when renewal becomes a permanent condition of school life.

I believe that current and aspiring school principals, teachers, and district and state officials will find this book immediately applicable to their efforts at renewing their own schools. This book is also for parents and guardians, other community members, businesspeople, and government officials, who should all be part of this vital enterprise.

In this book, I narrate what I have gleaned from years of working closely with public schools. Writing a book is a self-centered exercise; the most a reader can do is muse or, if angry, put the book away. One cannot interrupt or debate with the author. I appreciate the reader's willingness to indulge me, and I hope that his or her curiosity, discomfort, or anger will become a point of departure in the enduring renewal of every school in America.

Acknowledgments

I am indebted to many friends and colleagues who have collaborated with me on school renewal over the years. I will mention only those who have worked with me most recently, but

I thank all the other school practitioners and university educators in the United States, Canada, and Western Europe who allowed me to participate with them in their schools. I also wish to acknowledge Karen Allen, Lew Allen, Al Buccino, Emily Calhoun, Melba Dean, Richard Hayes, Frances Hensley, Barbara Lunsford, Nancy Quintrell, Jo Roberts, Kathleen Szuminski, and Russ Yeany for helping to make the League of Professional Schools and the Program for School Improvement a long-term reality. In addition, Donna Bell, Joe Blase, Ray Bruce, Jim Conkwright, Linda Darling-Hammond, Sara Orton Glickman, Bruce Joyce, Judy Lance, Ann Lieberman, Ed Pajak, Anita Peck, Jim Puckett, Werner Rogers, Ann Seagraves, Mike Short, Art Sills, Joel Taxel, and George Thompson provided insightful reviews and assistance with early drafts of the manuscript. I would also like to thank Jossey-Bass Publishers, BellSouth Foundation, the Georgia Leadership Academy, the National Diffusion Network, and the University of Georgia for their ongoing support.

Athens, Georgia   Carl D. Glickman
January 1993

The Author

Carl D. Glickman is University Professor, professor of social foundations of education, and chair of the Program for School Improvement at the University of Georgia. He received his B.A. (1968) from Colby College, M.A. (1970) from the Hampton Institute, and his Ed.D. (1976) from the University of Virginia. He has been a principal of award-winning schools, author of a leading academic text on school leadership, recipient of the outstanding teacher award in the College of Education, chair of several policy task forces to revitalize the public purpose of higher education and public schools, and the recipient of several national leadership awards. For the past twelve years, he has been the founder and head of various university–public school collaborations, including the League of Professional Schools. These collaborations focus on school renewal through governance, action research, and democratic education. These efforts have been cited as among the most outstanding educational collaborations in the United States by the National Business–Higher Education Forum, the U.S. Department of Education, and the Merrow Group of the U.S. Public Broadcast System. His book *Revolutionizing America's Schools* is a companion set of personal essays about applying democracy to education.

Carl Glickman resides in Athens, Georgia, with his spouse Sara Orton Glickman, a public school teacher. They have two grown children, Jennifer and Rachel, son-in-law Volker Stapper, and granddaughter Lea. The Glickmans spend their summers in conversation, writing, and fishing in Vermont.

Renewing
America's Schools

Chapter One

Introduction: Recapturing the Essence of Schools

The pressure of exhilarating events, which until then had aroused in me a surprising level of energy, abruptly vanished, and I found myself standing bewildered, lacking the inner motivation for anyting at all, feeling exhausted . . . . I wasn't the only one with these strange feelings; many of my colleagues . . . felt the very same way. We realized that the poetry was over, the prose beginning; that the country fair had ended and everyday reality was back. It was only then that we realized how challenging and in many ways how unrewarding was the work that lay ahead of us, how heavy a burden we had shouldered . . . . Somewhere in the depths of this feeling lay fear: fear that we had taken on too much, fear that we wouldn't be up to the job, fear of our inadequacy; in short, fear of our very selves.

Václav Havel (1990)

The county fair should be over. The work ahead should be heavy, in many ways unrewarding, and resting on our shoulders if we are to recapture the essence of public schools. History has recorded the incessant public education reform movements and the innumerable innovations that were to "save our schools." Since the turn of the twentieth century, education reports have been commissioned by prestigious academies and organization, governors, and presidents, with predictable howling about the atrocious schooling of American students, the decline of knowledge and skills, and the inability of educators

1

to rectify conditions. In my professional lifetime alone, I have seen American education blamed for the Soviet Union's putting the first satellite into space, for Johnny's not being able to read, for our nation's being at risk, and for the decline of our economic competitiveness with other countries. I have seen many innovations developed and exhorted by reformers: program planning and budgeting systems, performance-based competency education, direct instruction, mastery learning, individualized instruction, open education, "back to basics," management by behavioral objectives, team teaching, differentiated staffing, merit pay, career ladders, teacher effectiveness training, nongraded schools, cooperative learning, whole-language education, strategic planning, quality circles, and, most recently, "restructuring," transformational outcomes, site-based management, and total quality management.

Whether you are old or new to education, I would guess that you have already experienced a bewildering number of "hot" innovations and read a series of commissioned reports and newspaper articles lambasting our schools. Aside from our tendency to want quick answers to long-term concerns, what is it with Americans and public education? Why is American public education, more than any other public institution, buffeted every three to six months by another bold innovation and one more round of directives from legislators, school boards, superintendents, governors, and other policy makers? Why can't Americans stay on course and build schools on bedrock foundations of essential principles? After all, we do know that the schools that succeed are those that are not susceptible either to the winds of faddism or to bankrupt traditions of little educational merit.

In this book, I hope to portray the present state of our schools accurately, describe the three-dimensional framework of successful schools, and show how public schools, with appropriate involvement and support of local communities and district and state agencies, can more fully realize their essential purpose. I will explain how American schools and the American public can stay the course in remaking public schools into moral and productive places for students.

How Bad Are American Schools?

Each generation justifies its uniqueness by claiming to live in either the best or, more usually, the worst of times. "Never before in history" is a nice phrase for a speaker or writer to use in flattering an audience with the uniqueness of its generation. "Society is failing," "Violence is at an all-time high," "Drugs are rampant," and "Communities are falling apart" are all claims that have been made about nearly every period. This is not to deny that we do have real trouble and problems in schools, communities, and the larger society that need immediate and sustained attention. Increasing numbers of adults and children live in inhospitable conditions intolerable to decent humans in a caring society. But let us turn now to the performance of public schools, putting headlines and hysteria aside for the moment and looking at the facts.

As unpopular as it is to say, our public schools are no worse today than before. In fact, our public schools are better in many ways (Bracey, 1991, 1992; Graham, 1992; Jaeger, 1992). Public schools are doing a better job for minority and poor children. More than 85 percent of our students earn a high school diploma or its equivalent, as opposed to fewer than 10 percent at the turn of the century. Furthermore, there has been no appreciable decline in the achievement, knowledge, or skills of today's students as compared with students of years past.

The older generation always wants to think that it was smarter, wiser, and better educated than the present generation, but it simply is not true. If only 30 percent of eleventh-grade students can recite dates and details about the greatest presidents, it is a good guess that only 30 percent of students thirty, fifty, or seventy years ago could do likewise. On frequent occasions, throughout the United States, I have asked audiences of educators, businesspeople, parents, and other community members to raise their hands if they thought their own children in public schools were receiving a better education than they did. On every occasion, almost all the parents in the audience raised their hands immediately. Nevertheless, if I were to ask the same people the more general question of whether public education is better or worse than when they attended school, they would probably respond that it is much worse. People tend to think that their own personal experience with their own children in public schools is atypical, and they accept the general perception of calamity (Elam, Rose, and Gallup, 1992).

If American education is really no worse than before, and perhaps even better, then why does it receive so much bad publicity? It is because virtually every member of the general public has experience with a school as a student and can therefore be an "expert" on everyone else's school. Schools are the most public of our governmental institutions. They gobble up proportionally more of property owners' taxes than any other government service does and thus serve as a visible irritation and as the perennial "whipping boy" for our society when it gets down on itself. When American society works well, Americans do not applaud their schools; they applaud themselves. They extol the American spirit, the can-do economy, the courageous people, and the heroic leaders. When American society does not do well, they lambaste the schools.

It is absurd to believe the public rhetoric and the reports that claim American schools are behind the nation's decline. Are American schools responsible for the economic revival of Japan and Germany? Did American schools create the savings and loan scandal, the junk bond debacle, and the decline of the steel, auto, and computer industries? Schools do not create violence, family disintegration, environmental abuse, and neglect of children. In other words, public schools have not undermined the nation's health, as so many reports indicate; rather, the truth is that the nation has let children and schools down, and this is where the justified alarm goes off.

Schools are in trouble. There are increasing numbers of ill-fed, ill-clothed, ill-cared-for children, whose constant condition in life is grim and hopeless poverty. In a nation of local, state, and federal governments, the lack of attention to and intervention in these conditions has led to the increase of poverty among children. The result has been strain, tension, and an inadequate response on the part of educators and schools. To put it simply, schools are as good, on the whole, as they ever were; the percentage of children who have health-related, emotional, and social problems has increased significantly; and many schools now do have a more difficult time successfully educating such children. In other words, expectations and challenges for American public schools to educate all children have been raised to a new level.

Cutting the Hysteria but Being Real

One might think, from all the reports and newspaper articles about the poor performance of American youngsters and the rampant violence and use of drugs in American schools, that one's life would be imperiled by a visit to a public school. In fact, some of my guests from other countries have been literally afraid to visit schools that I worked with. After I convinced them to come and see these public schools in action, they were amazed to find students, teachers, volunteers, and administrators going about their business in a friendly and normal manner. Fights did not break out, classrooms did not look chaotic, drugs were not being injected in hallways, and students and adults treated one another with civility and respect.

Most elementary, middle, and secondary schools in the United States are neither imperiled nor life-threatening institutions. They are not very different from the schools that other generations of Americans have attended. The student population may be more diverse with respect to race, ethnicity, language, and socioeconomic level, but most schools are simply schools. Of course, there are schools where danger is omnipresent and the environment is out of control, but these are not the norm.

Today's rural schools have the same feeling as rural schools of the past. Today's suburban schools, although somewhat more racially diverse and less wealthy in terms of student population, generally have the same feeling as suburban schools of the past. The greatest change has been in inner-city public schools, which in the past were the best-funded and most prestigious public schools. Now, many inner-city schools are ill-kept, largely seg-

regated institutions. Many middle- and upper-class families have
continued to move to the suburbs, leaving behind people who
are generally poor, in communities with poor school facilities
and resources.

When I began teaching, in the 1960s, there were excellent public schools, mediocre public schools, and horrible public schools. Such schools could be found in rural, urban, and
suburban areas. I am confident that the same range could have
been found in 1880, 1910, 1930, 1950 and can be found today.
Georgia, where I live, is not particularly noted for the excellence of its public schools. Nevertheless, visitors from Austra-
lia, New Zealand, Germany, Korea, and Canada have traveled
here to visit some particularly good schools and have remarked
that these are comparable to the most advanced, enlightened,
and sophisticated public or private schools that they have seen
elsewhere. I am confident that the same could be said of some
public schools in every part of the United States.

The great problem of American public education is not
that public schools are as horrible as they are often portrayed
to be in the media; very few actually are. The problem of public education is its ordinariness. The issue is not how to lift public
schools out of disaster. Instead, the issue is how to allow great
schools to carry on, enable ordinary schools to strive for great-
ness, and provide initiatives and support for inept schools to
move toward competence. The first, erroneous perception —
that public education is mired in disaster — gets the attention.
The second, more accurate perception — that schools are ranged
along a continuum of ordinariness — needs the real work.

We can get on with this work only if we take the long view,
building public schools' internal capacity to excel and linking external assistance and resources to that internal work. We need
to cut the hype, shed the slogans, dismantle the quick innovations, and put the responsibility for good education where it be-
longs: in each school. We will not be able to improve, sustain,
and renew public education with yet another cycle of bandwa-
gons, quick fixes, and pendulum swings, for to do so would be
to do what we have always done, and the result would be the
same: ordinariness. What we need to do is reestablish the foundation of public schools and stick to first principles in education.

Paradox of Conservative Principles

This book will describe an extremely radical but readily attainable way to improve and renew virtually every public school and school district in the United States. As a director of school improvement programs, I have studied and worked with hundreds of public schools that have become purposeful and productive educational environments for their students. These schools have ranged in size from two hundred to three thousand students. In some, nearly all the students lived in poverty. In others, nearly all the students were affluent. They lived in rural, suburban, and urban regions. What I will describe is achievable, and there are schools throughout the United States and Canada that are living evidence.

The paradox in the ideas about to be proposed is that they are now sacred and conservative, but they were once the radical ideas that led to the formation of the United States. As such, they should undergird the remaking of our society and the role of public education in a democracy. We need to go backwards in order to go forward.

Recapturing the Goal of American Public Schools

For schools to rise to society's new expectations, it must be clear what those expectations are. Unfortunately, part of the reason why schools are such easy targets for criticism is that their goals are so diffuse and fragmented. We read that schools should have goals that address basic skills, self-esteem, vocational skills, higher-order thinking, health and nutrition, character education, responsible and cooperative behavior, aesthetic appreciation, and so on. With such diffuse goals, it is obvious that schools will not do as well on some. In the business sector, for example, goals are much simpler and more narrow; it is clear when a computer company does well. Likewise, when an enterprise in the public sector has clear goals, the results are apparent, and support is readily seen. Take the International Red Cross: a natural disaster occurs, people and resources are mobilized to save the victims, and the larger community congratulates the organization for its work and continues to support it.

The problem with schools is that it is not clear what primary and essential goals should stand as measures of success. Instead, different interest groups vie for schools' attention. When the goal of one group is accomplished well, another group lambastes the school for not doing better on its goal. The only way to rectify this situation is to make it clear that there is only one primary goal for American public schools: to return to its essence and prepare its students to become productive citizens of our democracy.

One might quibble with the wording, but the significant elements are there: *citizenship* and *democracy*. The goal of American schools is not to be first internationally in mathematics or science, or to teach basic skills or critical thinking, or to graduate students from high school. At best, these are subgoals of the larger, single goal of public education. When subgoals are treated as primary goals, they lead to fragmentation, vulnerability, and despair as schools try to be all things to all people. If a school emphasizes basic skills, it is criticized for not doing better on self-esteem or aesthetic appreciation. If a school emphasizes aesthetics and critical thinking, it is criticized for not spending more time on basic skills. With so many primary goals, and without a core to its existence, the public school cannot deliver.

What is needed is a return to the reason why common schools were established in the first place, why such schools were publicly funded, why the Constitution delegated control of public education to the states, and why an educated citizenry was essential to the working of the Constitution and the Bill of Rights. The value that unites Americans as a people, regardless of religion, culture, race, gender, life-style, socioeconomic class, or politics, is a belief in "government of the people, by the people, and for the people." Public education is the only institution designated and funded as the agent of the larger society in protecting the core value of its citizens: democracy.[1]

The essential value of the public school in a democracy, from the beginning, was to ensure an educated citizenry capable of participating in discussions, debates, and decisions to further the wellness of the larger community and protect the individual right to "life, liberty, and the pursuit of happiness." An educated citizenry and a democracy were one and the same, the lack of one would imperil the other.[2] Where the public school has strayed is in its loss of focus on this central goal.

What difference does it make if we graduate 100 percent of our students, or if SAT scores rise twenty points, or if our students beat other countries in achievement in science when they have not learned how to identify, analyze, and solve the problems that face their immediate and larger communities? Our country would be better served by schools that produce caring, intelligent, and wise citizens who willingly engage in the work of a democracy than by schools that produce graduates who do well on isolated subgoals.

If our schools can recapture their essence, then the expectations and indicators of success will become clearer and our schools will have a moral compass. Is it more alarming that fewer than 50 percent of tenth graders can write a fully cogent and grammatically correct letter or that only 17 percent of people between eighteen and twenty-four registers to vote (the lowest rate among all sectors of the U.S. population)? ("If Everyone Eligible Voted . . . ," 1992). If our schools were to focus on the main goal of citizenship and democracy and show students how to connect learning with the real issues of their surroundings, then more students would learn how to write cogent compositions, would learn basic skills, would use higher-order thinking, would learn aesthetic appreciation, would excel in academics, and would graduate. These secondary goals would be accomplished more readily as by-products of learned participation and responsibility. The reason why many of our students do not do better in schools is not that they are deficient, or that their teachers are incompetent or uncaring; the reason is that these students do not see the relevance of such learning to altering and improving their immediate lives in their communities. For them, school learning is a bore or, as one astute student told me, "a hassle you put up with during the day until you can return to the real world." If the central goal of schools were to prepare students to engage productively in a democracy, then this student, with his peers and teachers, would be working on the concerns of his immediate and future life and on the concerns of his immediate and extended communities. He would be learning to converse and study, read and write, and understand mathematics, science, art, and music in order to gain the power to make a better life for himself and his community.

A cynic might say, "That is all well and good for under-achieving and poor students, but what does this 'citizenship and democracy' notion have to do with students from highly edu-cated and wealthy homes who do well in school?" The answer is the same. Academically, most privileged students in our public schools do as well as, if not better than, previous generations. Nevertheless, in the absence of the school's central mission, there is only a pro forma experience of doing well, acquiring high grades, and entering a good college so as to get on eventually with life. School for these students is simply a pleasant enough stop on the way to the good life, not an experience that challenges and demands their full mental, emotional, and aesthetic involve-ment. To be blunt, public education without the central goal of democracy and citizenship is a hollow experience that serves no one well. The ultimate losers are all of us.

The most conservative idea today — protecting freedom in a democracy — was the most revolutionary idea at its incep-tion. Apathy in the United States and the isolation of students from the life of society are partly the result of our schools' for-getting their essential mission. Public schools that recapture it can move with a fervor, excitement, and engagement that set them apart from the ordinary and the mundane.

A Dangerous Opportunity

If you are a principal, teacher, paraprofessional, parent, stu-dent, community person, district official, school board mem-ber, or policy maker, I regret that the task about to be described is not glamorous. I regret that I cannot portray a quick and simple way to raise schools to new heights. It is hard and some-times explosive work.

Public education has entered a dangerous time, when its very existence is being questioned. There is another reform movement building momentum under the rubric of "choice" and "vouchers." The choice-and-voucher movement would erase the line between private and public schools, eliminate districts and school boards, and allow every school, private or public, to compete in the free-enterprise system of supply and demand. The process of decentralization, the effort to shed bureaucracies, and the importance of eliminating uniformity and regulations in order to renew public education will be detailed in this book.

In advocating the local school as the site for decision making and resource allocation, I may appear to agree with the proponents of decentralization through choice and vouchers. This is not true. The aim of choice-and-voucher systems — to allow all schools to compete individually — would represent further distancing of education from its common and core goal of fostering citizenship in a democracy and would lead to greater emphasis on subgoals. I believe that we need public schools as districts, school boards, and states strive for the common good. As such, they must be qualitatively different, both in their aims and in their support, from private schools.[3]

The choice-and-voucher movement has correctly pointed out that public schools are too inflexible and are unable to move quickly in responding to new demands (or, rather, responding to an old mission in dramatically changed circumstances). The move to site-based schools, with decision making and resource allocation done at the individual level, has been hastened by the choice movement. In some cases, those of us who have fought for greater autonomy and responsibility for individual schools now have it.

Before the verdict on the alleged failure of public education comes in, we have a chance, in this decade, to seize an opportunity to show what good people can do in a good institution. After a decade of legislated reform, bureaucratic control, standardization of work, and external decisions for improving schools, we are shifting toward an unfettering of the system, allowing schools to be different and encouraging site-based autonomy and responsibility. The choice-and-voucher movement has helped to decentralize reforms. Before it dismantles public education, those who believe in public schools, public school districts, and community-elected school boards want the time to show what can happen if every school is given the support, structure, and opportunity to act. The opportunity exists, the challenge is great, and the consequences are profound.

Ordinary Good People Doing
Extraordinary Good Work

In the latter part of this book, I will discuss the state and national policies that we will need in staying the course of the renewal of public schools. In Chapter Two, we begin with what we have: people in our public schools, with limited time and resources, trying to do their best in constrained conditions. We will move into the "skin" of a public school, lay out the three-dimensional framework of school renewal, and learn how operations and activities can be changed to afford good education to all students.

Part One

A Framework
for Renewing Schools

Chapter Two

The Covenant: Establishing Common Principles of Teaching and Learning

Any successful organization, whether it is a community or a religious, social, business, or educational group, has a set of core beliefs that holds its individual members together. That set of beliefs transcends any one person's self-interest. In the long run, the core beliefs help the group accomplish its mission and fulfill the needs and aspirations of individuals. The transcendent beliefs of successful groups do not simply force individual members to comply with the group; rather, they are developed from the members' ability to accomplish together what they could not do alone. Group goals become the ultimate fulfillment, both of the collective and of the individual. In other writings, I have referred to this core of the successful organization as "a cause beyond oneself" (Glickman, 1990b).

Commitment to the greater good harnesses the energy, resources, and activities of individuals in a purposeful manner. It is important, however, not to define such a collective and successful organization as necessarily moral or good. Successful organizations are also involved in criminal, discriminatory, and other harmful activities. If success is the group's accomplishment of its intended purposes, then success is neutral in the realm of higher values. A good *school,* however, is a successful organization that strives to realize the higher values involved in preparing productive citizens for a democracy.

15

Schools as Successful Organizations

Those who live in and around schools may not be aware that schools are unique organizations. Unlike other institutions, schools have little control over the composition of their clientele and little control over their resources and activities. Educators are in an occupation that does not display the characteristics of a profession. Furthermore, there is little time scheduled consciously for deliberations on meeting organizational goals.

I am defining successful schools as those that have set educational goals and priorities and accomplished them over time. These include goals for student achievement, grades, attendance, climate, self-esteem, prevention of vandalism, retention, postschool success, and parental and community satisfaction. Some findings about successful schools have received scant attention in the past, probably because of their unconventional nature:

Finding 1: Faculty in successful schools are less satisfied with regard to their teaching than are faculty in the less successful schools. In a forerunner study to the effective-school research, a constant degree of dissatisfaction with current teaching and learning was found to be central to success (Brookover, Beady, Flood, Schweiter, and Wisenbaker, 1979).

Explanation: In organizations whose members are always questioning existing practices, a desire to rectify inadequacies is created. There are schools where teachers applaud themselves and speak to others of how good or great they are, displacing energy into public relations and self-aggrandizement and diverting themselves from the work of making their schools better educational environments. A sense of dissatisfaction with current practices and organization is not a weakness; it is a strength of successful schools.

Finding 2: Successful schools are places where faculty members supervise and guide one another, plan courses together, and work in coordination. One of the most comprehensive studies of secondary schools found that the most glaring contrast between the most successful and the least successful schools concerned individual autonomy (Rutter, Maughan, Mortimore, Ouston, and Smith, 1979).

Explanation: In successful schools, faculty do not have a great deal of individual autonomy. They do not shut their classroom doors and teach in whatever ways they desire. A successful school achieves its goals and objectives through an accumulation of consistent practices. Unsuccessful schools, by contrast, have individual teachers who are left alone, who stay away from one another, and who do largely what they choose to do. If faculty members do not coordinate their efforts and plan an alignment of students' experiences, they tend, in their individual autonomy, to cancel one another's efforts.

Finding 3: In successful schools, faculty members are not treated as subordinates but instead are regarded as the colleagues of administrators and others involved in decisions and actions. In their controversial book advocating school choice, Chubb and Moe (1990) found that the most successful schools in America were those that had the greatest degree of site-based autonomy, where teachers were key participants in decisions.

Explanation: Successful schools exercise collective autonomy, apart from external agencies (districts, school boards, state departments), in making professional decisions about matters of schoolwide teaching and learning. Faculty members willingly decrease their individual autonomy in their own classrooms, in order to gain greater collective autonomy in the school.

Finding 4: Faculty members, administrators, and others in successful schools have established norms of collegiality for discussing and debating the big questions about how to constantly renew and improve the educational environment for all students.

Explanation: Successful schools are places where the larger questions about educational practice are constantly kept in the forefront of meetings and conversations (Rosenholtz, 1989). The words "what we should do for our students" are more typical than "what I will do for my students" or "what I as a principal want for my faculty" (Little, 1982). Successful schools have replaced condescending parochial, paternal, or maternal attitudes with earnest and serious discussion about what the members of a school community should be doing together for students.

Finding 5: Successful schools seek, produce, and consume information, and they see educational renewal as a continuing process, not as an event. Successful schools are always in the mode of change and renewal. They watch other successful schools at work and keep abreast of the research on topics and activities being considered. They collect data on their students and educational programs, and thus they set priorities that are based on thoughtful study.

Explanation: Most schools' goals and priorities are afterthoughts to external directives for school plans. Such goals and priorities usually come from the decisions of a few individuals or from surveys of what faculty members "feel" are the strengths and weaknesses of the school. Successful schools do not deal at the cardiac level. They expand their knowledge base by seriously studying their students and programs and by considering outside information before making schoolwide decisions. Successful schools know that school renewal is a continuing, everyday occurrence (Fullan and Miles, 1992). How to educate students better is regarded as a perennial question, always worth the time and energy its answer needs.

Traditions of Isolation

What do we have in these five findings about successful schools? We have what has always been known. Successful schools are places where adults strive — together, without hierarchical status — to answer the critical question of how to educate students better. The answer transcends any individual, can never be answered once and for all, and is the reason for uncovering and using as much information as possible before spending finite time and resources.

It is important to acknowledge that what appears to be common sense is very difficult and challenging to implement in the schools. Some schools have risen to the challenge of forging a collective good, but many more are still in the process. In others, the task is to begin to understand and discuss some rudimentary beginnings.

Our public schools are not normatively collective, purposeful, achievement-oriented institutions held in high regard by students, parents, community members, and educators themselves. Why is this so? Let me discuss some of the reasons, as follows (Glickman, 1990a).

Physical Organization to Keep People Apart

If one were to build a structure whose purpose was the promotion of uncoordinated activities, it would look like the typical school. It would be what we have — an eggcrate structure, with one teacher to approximately twenty or thirty students, each teacher boxed off from the others and unable to see the others at work, all without common times for informal or formal meetings.

Legacy of the One-Room Schoolhouse

The American public school of today was derived from the one-room schoolhouse of pioneer times. Teaching was the province of one person, who worked with students within four walls. Individual teaching autonomy is a tradition, carried forward in most current schools, where each teacher operates one classroom. The one-room schoolhouse is repeated every few yards, all the way down the hall.

Inversion of Responsibility

Beginning teachers tend to be given the least desirable physical spaces for their classrooms, the least adequate teaching materials and supplies, and, often, the most challenging students. The message to neophytes is that if they triumph over the initial hardships, then they can move on to a better and less challenging situation by passing the toughest demands on to the next generation of beginners.

In most other professions, the most experienced and com-

petent people handle the most challenging situations. In teaching, the legacy of protecting and bettering one's own "one-room
schoolhouse" creates an inversion of responsibility.

Restricted Dialogue

Two of the largest studies of American education indicate that
while teachers have virtual autonomy in deciding what and how
to teach, they have virtually no say at all when it comes to decisions about teaching and learning across classrooms, grade
levels, and departmental boundaries (Boyer, 1983; Goodlad,
1984). Most such decisions are made by people external to classrooms and schools. The 1980s came to be known as the era of
legislative reform in education because of incessant top-down
decisions of administrators, central offices, school boards, state
departments, legislatures, and governors about how schools and
teachers would operate (Darling-Hammond and Snyder, 1992).

Lack of Professional Dialogue

Most educators do not discuss teaching practices with one another except in contrived situations (see Grimmett, Rostad, and
Ford, 1992). Such matters rarely form the content of faculty
meetings, lounge or hallway conversations, or telephone calls.
Principals and teachers are more comfortable discussing students, parents, sports events, or community matters than discussing such issues as the curriculum, teaching strategies, staff
development, and student learning.

Restricted Access to Communication

Most schools are more comparable to the "mom and pop" grocery
stores of the 1930s than to the supermarkets of the 1990s when
it comes to communication access. In gathering information,
most teachers do not have the technology or the time to communicate outside or across their own classrooms. It is now common
for most professionals to have, at the minimum, a computer
and a modem for easy access to other people, files, and resources.

Most teachers, however, do not even have telephones in their classrooms. They usually have to wait patiently in school offices even to make simple phone calls to students' parents.

Existing Conditions as a Forum for Discussion: Types of Organizations

The existing conditions of schools are derived from traditions, rather than from sinister conspiracies to keep people isolated. Schools are less than fully effective, but not because educators are uncaring. There are very few teachers and administrators who take or even have coffee breaks or spend their school time in idle leisure. The overwhelming majority of school people work extremely hard, without great compensation and in stressful conditions, and they strive to do the very best they can for their students. School people are often caught unwittingly in structures and conventions that are counterproductive to the improvement of teaching practice. These are good people, trying to do good work (and becoming tired and at times discouraged), who simply cannot make the existing system work any better for themselves or their students (see McNeil, 1988; Sizer, 1984). The issue becomes one of building a school community where members have an opportunity to rethink the existing organization and decide on the level of energy and activity at which they wish to change schoolwide teaching and learning practices. This issue is not be taken lightly: as people rethink their organization and its purpose, function, and activities, they move outside the secure and the known. While changing students' lives, they will be changing their own lives as well. In my own work with schools that are engaged in such rethinking, the experience is both exhilarating and painful. Once begun, it is hard to turn back.

Table 2.1 shows three types of school organization: conventional, congenial, and collegial.[1] *Conventional* schools are characterized by the one-room schoolhouse mentality: autonomy for the individual teacher, small cliques of teachers within the school who befriend one another, lack of dialogue across classrooms and levels about teaching, and a school site seen

Table 2.1. Types of Schools.

Conventional	Congenial	Collegial
Isolated	Social	Professional respect; personal caring as a by-product of work
Individual teacher's autonomy	Individual teacher's autonomy	Collective autonomy
School seen as physical site for work	Pleasant and open climate for adults	Purposeful conflicts, resolution on behalf of students

mostly as a physical place of work. *Congenial* schools are characterized by an open, social climate for adults. Communications are friendly, and teachers, parents, caretakers, and principals easily socialize with one another. Faculty meetings are pleasant, holiday parties are great, refreshments at meetings are plentiful, and faculty members spend time together away from school (aerobics on Thursday night, stress-management workshops). Members describe their school as a nice place where everyone gets along well. *Collegial* schools are characterized by purposeful, adult-level interactions focused on the teaching and learning of students. People do not necessarily socialize with one another, but they respect their differences of opinion about education. Mutual professional respect comes from the belief that everyone has the students' interest in mind. The result of such respect is seen in school meetings, where the school community members debate, disagree, and argue before educational decisions are made. Even in the hottest of debates, people's professional respect for others supersedes personal discomfort. People believe that differences will be resolved and that students will benefit. Social satisfaction is a by-product of professional engagement and resolution, of seeing how students benefit, and of the personal regard in which adults hold one another. They become colleagues in the deep sense of being able to work and play together, and each side of the relationship strengthens the other. Being collegial means being willing to move beyond the social facade of communication, to discuss conflicting ideas and issues with candor, sensitivity, and respect. For many schools, the first job is to move from being conventional to being congenial, but the big job for public education is to become collegial, so that social satisfaction is derived mainly from the benefits derived from efforts on behalf of students.

Without a clear understanding of the primary goal of schools — fostering citizenship in a democracy — and an ensuing covenant of teaching and learning, a school may easily take on greater collective decision making, building a structure and making time for it, but still be no better a place for students. Instead, people may make decisions that improve the lives of adults (a better adult climate, more socially cohesive activities) rather than making decisions that improve teaching and learning. Ultimately, the aim is to have a school environment that fulfills students' needs and, in doing so, fulfills adults' needs as well.

Developing the Covenant

The idea that public education and democracy are intertwined creates the central goal of American public schools. For schools to be true to that goal, procedures and processes for its accomplishment must be democratic. This point touches on the glaring hypocrisy of public school operations and on why policy makers have fallen short in sustaining strategies and reforms for improving education. Most policies in public education are undemocratic in their creation and implementation. Policies are not decided by those who will be affected, do not represent the people in the school community, and are not derived from the vision of the people. Most ideas in education derive from power, popularity, or novelty. These ideas temporarily hold sway, but within a few years they pass away and become tried innovations that failed. Then critics have yet another field day with the failure of the public schools.

For school renewal to endure, every school and district in our land needs principles that transcend the interests of any individual and that are derived from constituents. These principles must be congruent with a definition of the core values of a democracy: freedom, justice, and equality *as well as* life, liberty, and the pursuit of happiness for all. These principles will not be swayed by politics, fads, or special interests. Such a covenant, rather than taking up space in a policy book or passing someone else's inspection, is a living embodiment of why we as a school community do what we do. It becomes the screen for saying "Yes, we do that here" or "No, we will not do that here."

I use the word *covenant* purposely here, to describe learning principles that are derived from a definition of education and democracy and that are more than a vision of teaching and learning. A vision is what we would like to imagine; a covenant is a sacred obligation to spend a life in accordance with it. A covenant should be reconsidered and revised periodically, but it is where a school plants its feet, the place from which it will not be moved. From it emanate a mission, goals, and plans.

There are many ways and sequences for establishing a covenant, but the important thing is that the covenant (1) be derived from all the people who are affected (students, parents, staff, administrators, and others, such as community members and business partners); (2) be derived through a democratic process, whereby no one makes decisions for everyone else; (3) be focused solely on teaching and learning and what teaching and learning should look like in the particular school; and (4) be a guide for future decisions about school priorities with respect to such matters as staff, schedules, materials, assessment, the curriculum, staff development, and resource allocation.

Principles of Learning

The following principles illustrate such a covenant. These were drawn up by a local group that involved students, parents, educators, community members, and businesspeople (Teaching and Learning Task Force, 1991). The question that guided discussion was "What should learning look like in an optimal educational environment?" Consensus was reached after a series of meetings over six weeks.

1. Learning should be an active process that demands full student participation in pedagogically valid work. Students need to make choices, accept responsibility, and become self-directed.

2. Learning should be both an individual and a cooperative venture, where students need to work at their own pace and performance levels and also have opportunities to work with other students on solving problems.

3. Learning should be goal-oriented and connected to the real world, so that students understand the applications of what they learn in school to their outside lives and communities.

4. Learning should be personalized, to allow students, together with their teachers, to set learning goals that are realistic but challenging, attainable, and pertinent to their future aspirations.

5. Learning should be documentable, diagnostic, and reflective, providing continuous feedback to students and parents, to encourage students and train them in self-evaluation. Assessment should be used as a tool to develop further teaching and learning strategies.

6. Learning should take place in a comfortable and attractive physical environment and in an atmosphere of support and respect, where students' own life experiences are affirmed and valued and where mistakes are analyzed constructively as a natural step in the acquisition of knowledge and understanding.

Another covenant for teaching and learning can be adapted from the methodology advocated by the Foxfire Teacher Network (see Appendix A). Students in every classroom, staff members at faculty meetings, and parents and community members at evening meetings are given the same individual task: to describe their most memorable learning experiences. After reminiscing, writing, and narrating in small groups, people are then asked to determine the underlying principles of learning that were common to their most memorable learning experiences. The final step is to ask representatives of each group to come together and determine what learning should look like so that the school can be filled with memorable learning experiences for students.

Each school will need to adjust the questions and procedures to its own context. Several other questions could also be used for deriving a covenant: How do you learn best? What would teaching and learning look like in the ideal classroom or school? If you could learn in any way that you wanted, how would you go about it? (Of course, very young children, as well as others who have difficulty writing, will have to be able to narrate their ideas to an adult, an older student, or a volunteer.) Schools where parents or caretakers do not usually attend meetings may have to be sampled and surveyed by correspondence, phone, or personal visit, or representative parents can be invited to attend a special coffee hour. Students themselves could develop interview protocols and survey grandparents and businesspeople. There is no single way of developing such principles, but they should be derived through a democratic process conducted by those affected. They should focus on teaching and learning and guide later actions.

What has been interesting for me in conducting this type of exercise with various schools is how remarkably alike the lists of principles are. People of various political persuasions, economic levels, races, cultures, and ages tend to see optimal learning in generally similar terms. Nevertheless, the differences create insight and discussion, and resolving them contributes to the uniqueness of each school.

What to Do with the Covenant

After deriving a covenant through a democratic process (more details on school-based democratic procedures will be found in the next chapter), the school now has a framework for comparing desired learning in principle with current day-to-day practice. In such discrepancy checks, a school may immediately find that certain practices (teaching methods, materials, allocation of instructional time, grouping of students, grading and evaluation practices over the normal course of a day) are consistent with the covenant, while others simply are not. It will probably become obvious that there is a need to study what actually happens to students during their school day—what they learn, and how they go about learning.

The structure for school renewal must be built first, to provide a firm shelter for the "inside" work. One side of the three-part framework—the covenant—has now been constructed. The other two sides—the charter, and the critical study process—remain.

Chapter Three

The Charter:
Understanding How
Decisions Are Made

Educators cannot teach students how to gain entry into the knowledge and power of the profound discussions of a democracy unless they themselves have gained entry into the knowledge and power of the profound discussions of their schools. Faculty, staff, and administrators need to learn and relearn that their students do not belong to them. Fourth-grade teachers do not possess their fourth-grade students; eleventh-grade history teachers do not own their eleventh-grade students; sixth-grade English teachers do not hold their students. Students move to different teachers over the years, and some move among teachers during the day. For the length of their stay, students are members of the larger school community.

Successful schools and outstanding educators understand that they need not own students in order to fully educate them. To fully educate a student, teachers need to do their best during the temporary time together and to care just as much about the educational experiences that the student had before coming and the experiences that the student will have after leaving. To believe that the job of a classroom teacher is to operate solely in the present with his or her immediate charge is to deny a school the opportunity to provide a cumulative, purposeful effect. To focus on an individual classroom and on the present resigns students to a fragmented education. If I really care about the education of "my" kids, I have to care about them before and after me; thus, I need to view what is "mine" as "ours."

28

For students to belong to everyone, a school community—extending beyond teachers and administrators—must have a way to provide what is wanted for all of them. How does a school enact a covenant of the principles of learning? How can a school be democratic, focus on future learning, be nonpossessive, and still allow educators to work in the immediate present?

The Charter

A charter is an understanding of how decisions are to be made. It spells out who is to be responsible for what, the composition of decision-making bodies, the decisions to be made, and the process to be used. For example, how does a school decide on a covenant? What is the culminating process? In what follows, I will describe democratic procedures used in the public schools with which I have worked most recently. What is important to consider is not the particular model to be described, but rather the school's development of its own model consistent with democratic principles, appropriate to the organizational readiness of the school, and in line with the recent history of the school.

Guiding Rules of Governance

There are three guiding rules, as follows:

1. Everyone can be involved in decision making.
2. No one *has* to be involved.
3. Once decisions are made, everyone supports the implementation.

All those who are active members of a society and meet the criteria of citizenship should have the same vote as all other citizens. One's *right* to vote is not a *requirement* to vote, however. Citizens of our democracy are not legally required to vote, yet when the citizens make a decision, the individual, whether or not he or she participated, is bound to its implementation. In our own local town, if we decide not to vote in the next bond referendum on whether to raise taxes for a new sewage system, the decision (to raise our taxes) applies to us regardless of what we think about the issue. If later we say that we are not going to abide by the decision (and not pay the additional tax), then we must face the consequences of being disobedient with the legal decisions of our society.

The time to make our views known is during the decision-making process. Afterward, we can grumble and complain and try to have the decision reconsidered; in the meantime, we must abide by it.

The strength of having these guiding rules of governance in a school is that they do not force people to be involved in decisions that they may not have the time, interest, or energy for. Instead, they ask people to commit themselves to a process of decision making in which they can choose a level of participation. An individual who does not like a particular decision, but who chose not to be involved, will learn to become more involved in the future.

Locus of Control

To be effective, governance must deal with issues that are within people's power to rectify. Towns do not make decisions about other towns. The state of Minnesota does not make decisions about what the state of Vermont must do. Countries cannot pass laws and programs for other countries. By themselves, they can act only within their own spheres of direct, legal control. Schools, likewise, need to set up governance structures for what "we" can do in "our" own school with "our" own personnel and resources, within the policies of larger authorities.

In schools, the locus of control for decisions involves what *we* can do — not what *others* need to do — within the expanded parameters of authority and policies as allowed by the district and state. Without such clear delineation, schools tend to use governance to make decisions that transfer the onus of responsibility to others. A high school can easily spend its time making decisions about what the middle school should do. The middle school can choose to make decisions about what the elementary school should do. The elementary school can decide about what parents and daycare centers should do. This is the old game of "passing the buck down," which translates into "We are fine; the *real* problem with education happens before they come to us." Another old game is called "passing the buck up." The elementary school makes decisions for the middle school, the middle school for the high school, and the high school for the colleges and vocations. The message here is "We are fine; the *real* problem happens when they leave us." A third old game involves passing the buck to the community, the district, and the board. In this game, a school, regardless of its grade level, makes decisions about what the community, the district, or the board need to do for it. The decisions are for more community programs, more money and additional personnel from the district, and changed board policies. The message of this game is "We are fine; the *real* problems are with those outside agencies."

Unless a school develops and uses its governance process for issues that people in the school can do something about, governance becomes an occasion for bemoaning, complaining, and hand-wringing. The school community that does not want to look at itself can avoid doing so by blaming and shifting responsibility to others. Regardless of the particular game, the message is the same: "We are fine. We do not need to change. If only those others would do what we want them to do, everything would be all right." This game was understandable in the past, when most control over school decisions did not reside in the schools, but enduring school renewal demands that schools take responsibility and action for themselves.

There are important responsibilities that other schools, communities, and school districts must take on to support the capacity to improve. In a later chapter, we will discuss the need for coordination, decentralization, new district board and state policies, and venture capital. For now, the simple message is that a school community must decide for itself what type of teaching and learning place it wants to be. Since school people are so busy, the time they spend on governance should be spent on what can be done and attained, rather than on what cannot be controlled.

Focus of Governance

If a school is to foster educated citizenry for a democracy, then the school itself must be an example of a democracy. The substance of a democracy is the decisions that improve conditions of the society. The substance of a school democracy is the decisions that improve the education of students, both collectively and individually, and the quality of educational life for the entire school community. Therefore, the focus of decisions should always be the enactment of the covenant: how to enhance schoolwide teaching and learning.

An understanding of what is meant by a focus on teaching and learning is essential if a school is to be true to its covenant. The work of schools is teaching and learning for the higher purpose of productive democratic citizenship. When school community members spend most of their time on administrative, managerial, and adult convenience/congenial activities, they lose their sense of purpose. Table 3.1 shows the types of decisions that are most helpful in the school that is striving to be a democratic, educative community.[1]

Zero-impact decisions consume the time of most conventional and congenial schools and deal primarily with adult concerns. Decisions about parking spaces, lunchroom and hall supervision, adult recreation, and smoking in the teachers' lounge are not the primary reasons people aspire to become educators. One does not need specialized preparation in education to spend time figuring out what should go into the vending machines in the teachers' lounge or how the bus schedule duty roster should be handled. These matters do need to be dealt with, but in a manner that does not detract from decisions about education.

Minimal-impact decisions are about issues that do pertain to student learning but are of short duration and have less direct influence. Often such decisions do not change basic educational experiences for students but do update and coordinate existing activities. Examples of this type are how to plan the normal parent open houses, what to do during the two or three inservice days built into the year, what texts to order in the next adoption cycle, how to appropriate limited discretionary funds, or a

Table 3.1. Focus of Governance: Educational Impact.

Zero-Impact Decisions	Minimal-Impact Decisions	Core-Impact Decisions	Comprehensive-Impact Decisions
Parking spaces	Textbook adoption	Curriculum	School budget
Lunchroom supervision	Parent programs	Staff development	Hiring of personnel
Faculty lounge	In-service days	Coaching	Deployment of personnel
Sunshine fund	Small budgets	Instructional programs	Personnel evaluation
Adult recreation	Discipline policy	Student assessment	
Bus duties		Instructional budget	
Refreshments			

perennial one — how to better coordinate discipline policy in regard to inappropriate student behavior. These decisions usually do not change the fundamental teaching and learning practices in classrooms and across the school.

Core-impact decisions are those that enact the covenant, the core principles of teaching and learning. These are the long-term, sustained decisions that a school makes about curriculum, staff development, coaching of each other, instructional programs, assessing and reporting student learning, and the entire instructional budget (materials, time, and personnel). These decisions align the school with its educational values. A successful school that is purposeful and democratic uses most of its meeting time and governing structure to make these decisions.

Comprehensive-impact decisions involve broader issues than teaching and learning as such. They concern what is known as *site-based management.* Authority over the entire school budget, the hiring and employment of personnel, and personnel evaluation are decentralized by the district and state to give individual schools total control over their resources. Giving a school total autonomy to manage its resources will not necessarily improve education if the school has not dealt with core-impact decisions before attempting to deal with comprehensive-impact decisions.

Who Should Govern: The Ideal

The question of who should sit at the table and have an equal say in educational decisions is a complicated one. Ideally, all those involved in the educational enterprise of a school should have voting membership. Educational decisions at the school level will affect faculty, the principal, students, staff, paraprofessionals, parents and caretakers, other community members, businesspeople, district office personnel, and school board members. Furthermore, subgroups within each category of membership could be broken down even further. For example, faculty could be subdivided into regular classroom teachers, resource teachers, special education teachers, and other support personnel. They also could be subdivided by upper grade, lower grade, department, gender, years of experience, and so on. Such sub-division can be taken to impractical extremes, however.

Let me suggest, in the ideal, a few ground rules for membership in school governance groups:

1. All major groups should be represented, with access always open to others.
2. Regular classroom teachers should be in the majority.
3. The school principal should be a "standing" (automatically included) member.
4. The group as a whole should fairly represent the gender, ethnic, and socioeconomic populations of the entire school community.

Rule 1 means that the democratic process should be open to any member of the group (parent, teacher, community member, student), regardless of whether he or she has a formal role on an official governing board. There should be task forces and study groups, with formal solicitations for any interested persons to participate, and open hearings should be held before a formal governing board makes any important schoolwide decision. In this way, anyone in the school community can participate at some level and be heard.

Rule 2 is crucial to school renewal. Teachers should have the majority voice on all decisions affecting their professional work. The work of educators is education—implementing teaching and learning practices. I am aware that some disagree with the idea that teachers should have majority control. If teaching is to become a true profession, however, then teachers must be able to exercise the judgment that they have been prepared for: how to best teach, and how students should learn. It is only in allowing teachers to use their minds and collective judgment with other community members that we establish critical, thoughtful, and professionally alive places that retain, support, and attract thoughtful professionals. If educational decisions are to be made by a majority of citizens, laypeople, or noneducators, then we do not need educators. We should, then, logically eliminate all specialized preparation for teachers and simply hire people who are willing to follow other people's ideas on education. Giving noneducators control over educational decisions will not improve public schools. Nevertheless, some school issues are not primarily pedagogical, and they do call for greater control by noneducators. These include such issues as community values, school or community service programs, parent programs, afterschool programs, and use of community resources. In the parcelling out of areas of decision making with an eye to proper representation, a school finds overall clarity in its operations and consistency with its covenant.

Rule 3 means that the school principal should always be viewed as a critically important faculty member, with broad responsibility for overall coordination and articulation of school programs. Therefore, the principal is rightfully seen as a permanent member of the school's governing group. This does not necessarily mean that the principal formally convenes and presides over the governing group or has any greater influence than anyone else. Again, some argue the opposite. Principals should not be disenfranchised from the educational operations of teacher-run schools; instead, they should be seen as faculty members who have made the same career commitment as other faculty to improve education for students. In some places, adversarial conditions between principals and teachers (the management-labor dichotomy) have come about through the loss of the original idea of the principal as head *teacher* rather than head *administrator*. We can recapture the sense of principal and teachers as part of the same faculty only if those in education, regardless of their conferred roles, see one another primarily as educators, with the same care, concern, and right to make educational decisions.[2]

Rule 4 states that the group as a whole must reflect the diversity of the community. I hope that we will reach the day when such a rule need not be spoken but will simply be automatically understood and followed. If the school and the adult community represent certain proportions of ethnic and socioeconomic groups, then so should the governing board. If the school has a large percentage of students from low-income households, caregivers/parents from low-income households should be represented. If the school community has more women than men, then men should not be overrepresented on the governing board. When a school pays careful attention to the question of representation and thus gives each group a voice, educational decisions become, by definition, more sensitive to multicultural and socioeconomic factors.

Who Should Govern: The Reality

The ideal can be embraced all at once or in transitional steps over two or three years. This is where sensitivity to the school's readiness and prior history comes into play. For example, if a school's parent and community group has constantly played a role (positive or negative), then it would make sense to involve those people heavily in decisions about the governing board's composition. If a school has had a noticeable lack of parent or community involvement, it might be equally important to begin with an in-school governing board (consisting mostly of school personnel) and immediately commission a study or advisory group of invited parents and community members to recommend how the governing board might have greater parent or community representation within a few years.

The same holds true for students and central office personnel. Students should be represented in school governance (although to what degree is open to debate). A school with children under the age of twelve or thirteen will probably not expect children to be able to take full responsibility and exert equal influence with adults. Some discussions would be irrelevant to them, and the extra time demanded of them would be unproductive, but it would be appropriate if some topics brought up at the governance table went back to the students (or to the student council) for input and consideration. Students should also be able to tell the governing council about those educational issues that concern them. The older the students are, the more realistic it is for them to have actual representation in school governance. Regardless of the students' age, it is important for the school to offer students continuing opportunities to participate in decisions about learning activities, learning projects, learning assessments, learning contracts, proper decorum, and ethical and civic behavior.

The proper involvement of central office, district, and school board personnel is also complicated. Ideally, it would be best for at least one representative from the central office of a school district to be a member of the governance body of a local school. That person would not only voice her beliefs on matters of importance but also identify resources and information to assist the school. She could serve as a liaison to the district or board on matters that affected policies. The reality, however, is that in many districts there are not enough people who have the time, inclination, attitude, or expertise to serve as active, permanent members at all school meetings. Therefore, the compromise for many schools is an "unofficial" central office person who serves as the school's contact person and as a periodic consultant to the school. The role, organization, and policies of districts involved in supporting school renewal will be discussed further in later chapters.

The discussion of the gap between the ideal and the reality of composing a governing group in a school is about how to get started (the reality) and, eventually, about how the school wishes to be (the ideal). At the minimum, a school needs to start with a majority of school faculty and the principal, with active solicitation of paraprofessionals, students, parents, community members, and district personnel on particular issues. Eventually, a school's governance should include representatives of all the school's various constituencies.

What Type of Governance?

It might appear that all democracies in schools should be established and structured in the same way. This is not true. Schools need to make their own judgments as to the best way to proceed at any particular moment. What is true about our own democracy in the United States, and what will serve as governing rules for schools, is that everyone can be involved in decision making, no one has to be involved, and once decisions are made, everyone must comply with their implementation. If one does not like a particular decision, then one has the right to try to change it through the democratic process. Furthermore, built into the governing structure is a set of governing conditions: one person, one vote; no ultimate veto for any individual; a decision-making rule that finalizes decisions; and ratification of the process, structure, and decision-making rule by the body at large.

"One person, one vote" is self-explanatory. "No ultimate veto" means that, in a democracy, no one person can permanently stop the decisions of the group; an ultimate veto only occurs in totalitarian societies. If the governing process is to include veto power — on the part of the chair of the council, the principal, or some tribunal — it must be only a temporary one, susceptible to reversal by a vote of the larger group. "A decision-making rule" means that every citizen in a democracy knows beforehand what is the necessary vote to finalize a decision; it might be a simple majority, two-thirds, or consensus. Regardless of what it is, the rule is clear before groups get involved in the particular issues to be resolved. "Ratification" means that the responsibilities of members and groups, what they decide on and what they do not, and how final decisions are made are approved by a forum of the constituents before implementation. For example, in most of my recent work with public schools, we rely on an 80 percent affirmative vote, by secret ballot, of the total faculty *and* the clear support of the superintendent and the school board before a school can begin to use its governing process.

Representative, Direct, and Hybrid Governance

Democracies can be conceptualized in two forms — representational, and dependent on direct participation. A representative form means that members either volunteer or are elected to represent their constituents. They serve as members of the governing body or council that can make decisions on behalf of their constituents (se Figure 3.1). In such a structure, a certain number of representatives are elected or volunteer from the variously defined groups — teachers and counselors, paraprofessionals, students, parents, community groups, central office personnel — and they consider and make decisions for the rest of the groups.

Figure 3.1. Representative Form.

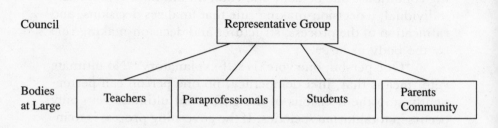

Council

Bodies
at Large

The "people" themselves have a voice in whom they elect to represent them. They may be consulted, at times, but they largely give their "say" to their representatives to decide for them.

A less used form of democracy is direct participation (see Figure 3.2). As in the town meeting, the "people" do not turn their "say" over to anyone, but keep it for themselves. When an issue comes under discussion, a convener announces a meeting time, and all those who wish to participate are invited to do so. Those who attend then decide priorities, indicate whether further study is needed, and agree on when the group as a whole will make a decision.

A common merger of the two forms of governance is one that includes a representative governing council for the overall identification of priorities, establishing of task forces, and setting of time lines for recommendations, but all final decisions go back to a direct referendum of the group as a whole. Most of the schools that I have worked with have developed and refined such a hybrid model.[3] Figure 3.3 depicts such a structure.

Figure 3.2. Direct Participation.

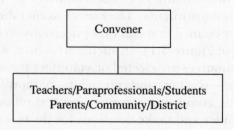

Figure 3.3. Hybrid Governance.

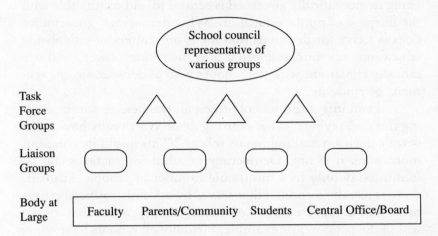

A school council is composed of elected members or volunteers (with the exception of the principal, who is an automatic member). The council establishes priorities and commissions task forces of volunteers (composed of faculty, students, parents, and others) to deliberate and make recommendations to the council. Once the task force makes its recommendation, its job is done. The council then studies the recommendation and asks each of its members to discuss the recommendation with liaison groups, for further input. Liaisons are all the members of the school community, organized into small groups, who serve as communication links to assigned council representatives. In this way, the council receives communication from the entire body about a recommendation. After such feedback, the school council, according to its decision-making rule, can either approve the recommendation or take it to the body at large for a final vote. A more specific example of a school charter is included in Appendix B.

Above the Details

It is easy to get lost in the details of democratic governance (although the details are important in the development and acceptance of the school's constitution) and lose the spirit of why being democratically governed is central to and compatible with the purpose of public education. What democratic governance does is strive for decisions that focus on matters of schoolwide education, are fair and equal and distribute power, and are morally consistent with the school's goal of democratic engagement of students.

I can imagine a school principal, teacher, or parent reading this and saying, "What's the big deal? We already have democratic decision making in our school." This might be true, but more often it is not. Democracy in adult interactions can be found today only in a minuscule number of schools. Instead, there is usually a council that serves by administrative appointment and is representative of management, rather than of the will of the people. For example, virtually all schools have some type of departmental, team, or grade-level leadership structure that is appointed by the principal. This is not what I am talking about. There is nothing wrong with such cabinets when they conduct administrative business and serve the interests of departments, grade levels, or teams, but they tend to fight, and rightfully so, for their domains. That is why they were appointed, and they are often politically controlled by their superordinates. What I am talking about is a governing structure of freely elected or volunteer members who represent the school across grade levels, departments, and community lines, with the sole mission of figuring out the best education for all children, regardless of the current organizational, grade-level, and departmental lines.

I can also imagine the same reader persisting in the idea that his or her school is "democratic," meaning that communication is open, people are listened to, and decisions are always made with carefully solicited input. Again, this is not what I am talking about. I mean schools where the authoritarian and dependency mantle, no matter how benevolent and caring, has been consciously dismantled because everyone knows that final decisions will be made in a manner by which every vote is equal, and those in status positions will have the same rights and responsibilities to influence decisions but, in the end, can win or lose as easily as anyone else.

Why Do This?

It is much easier to write about disrupting existing organizational patterns for making decisions than it is to actually do so. There are many conventional and congenial schools where students, faculty, parents, and administrators are operating well on a day-to-day basis. There is no great dissatisfaction with the operation. People go about their business, and decisions are made by an authority figure, by a small group of people, or by happenstance. Why would anyone in his right mind want a school organization to involve people in knowingly taking a critical look, raising the ante of professional dialogue, debate, and conflict, and giving up a secure structure? Furthermore, to develop the covenant and constitution takes time. Why should anyone expect faculty — a school's most valuable resource — to want to spend time in this way? Finally, why would a principal who has achieved a position of authority now want to distribute power equally and have the same vote as anyone else?

The answer is twofold. First, all democracies are ragged and inefficient. The same question — "Why do it?" — can be asked of society at large. Why do we defend and even die to protect such governance in our larger society? It is not efficient, it leads to debate and conflict, and it undermines the security of having an authority figure to decide for the people. The moral reason why a school community should be willing to take the plunge is that it is consistent for public education to operate by the premises it wishes to inculcate in its students: the maintenance and development of a democratic society. Second, a democratic school, over time, is a more satisfying and professionally rewarding place for students, faculty, and parents or guardians. It becomes a true community, and power given up by an individual becomes power gained by all. Some individuals are relatively comfortable giving up power. For others, the relinquishing of power has to be carefully learned and tested. The issue of time is the great sorter between those schools ready to plunge into democracy and those that need to take small steps.

A real frustration for teachers is figuring how to teach current students, keep up with day-to-day classroom responsibilities, and devote time to a schoolwide decision-making process.

A similar frustration for a principal is figuring out how to collaboratively establish a governance process, establish a covenant, identify priorities, and make changes and still deal with paperwork, fire drills, state requirements, and maintenance schedules. These reasons are real, but they can mask or become excuses for not going forward. A principal can say, "I am willing to share in decisions, but I do not have the time." Teachers can say, "Sure, we are willing to be involved, but we need more time."

Testing Commitment

Time for educators to plan with one another and their constituents is the scarcest resource in school renewal, but it should not be an obstacle for moving ahead. Some schools have more scheduled time, in terms of early-release days, planning days, faculty meetings, and joint planning periods. Other schools have more constraints, with scheduled faculty meetings as the only time available to meet.

The issue for teachers and principals who want to move ahead should not be "We do not have time to do this" but rather "With the time we have, at what level do we begin?" By reframing the question, we can now deal with what people are truly willing to do. At what level of decision making does a principal feel willing to give up authority and have one vote? At what level of decision making do teachers want to use their available time to be involved? What decisions should remain mainly administrative? Which ones should simply incorporate a process for input? Which ones are the most important, that all parties would wish to make democratically? This does not have to be an all-or-nothing affair. Instead, it can be a beginning.

The determination of the level and scope of decisions can be done in several ways (see Table 3.1). Faculty, principals, paraprofessionals, parents, and students, independently of each other, could identify areas of schoolwide educational decisions that they would want and be willing to share. Another way would be simply to ask, on a survey, that individuals write down the decisions to which they would give the highest priority. Still another way would be to have students, parents, community members, administrators, faculty, and paraprofessionals meet, review data on student progress, and agree on common activities that would represent the first decision areas for democratic governance. In my experience, many schools have developed and approved governance processes and covenants and then used the democratic process to decide on the topics, tasks, and issues to tackle.

How Formal Should Rules and Procedures Be?

What is the best decision-making rule to use for a school: majority vote, two-thirds, 80 percent, or consensus? The answer is for a school to decide and make part of its charter. There are schools that operate from a tradition of consensus — no school-wide educational decision is enacted until there is agreement on everyone's part. There are schools that use a two-thirds vote of the body at large, and there are those that use a simple majority vote. Some schools operate with more complex rules, such as consensus on the part of the school council; if consensus is not forthcoming, the decision is tabled for several weeks and then approved by a two-thirds vote. In my own work with public schools, I have insisted on an 80 percent vote of approval, by secret vote of the school community members, in order to ratify and begin. My reason has been that I wanted initially to work only with schools that had a strong commitment to embrace democratic school renewal. Schools can be successful by using majority vote or consensus, however. Obviously, the higher the percentage of approval, the more likely it is that the school will have total commitment. I believe that the ideal would be consensus, but I am fully aware that there are schools that, at least for the immediate term, would not be able to make any decisions if consensus were the rule. In these schools, a 50 percent vote would be a major achievement.

Therefore, in keeping with the idea that the process should be developed from within, a school must determine a reasonable decision-making rule (based on at least a majority) that shows more people for a decision than against it and that gives everyone the opportunity to participate, be heard, and influence the decision.

Does a school need a formal constitution and governing organization in order to be democratic? In the long term, maybe not; in the short term, probably yes. Some school organizations resist structures. The principal, teachers, parents, and students prefer to convene informally and make decisions as they go, without any covenant, charter, or clear decision-making rules. Such informality must be analyzed at two levels. At the first level, if school participants are asked individually about the informal decision-making process, and if each one can easily describe the same process of how democracy works, then the school has an extraordinarily enlightened process that does not need to be formalized in writing. At the second level, if participants are asked individually about their process, and if perceptions vary dramatically — ranging from "We always come to an agreement by consensus" to "The principal is always in the background and pulls strings to get his way" to "There is a small group of teachers and parents that manipulates the decisions" — then the informal process is not working, and a formal constitution is in order.

In my experience, democratic decision making is currently not prevalent in schools; norms of hierarchy, control, status, and power hold sway, in formal and informal ways. For norms of trust and equality to be established, clear and formal constitutions must be established (preferably in written form), so that everyone knows the process, violations are readily apparent, and revisions are readily made. A clear, formal process is not synonymous with a cumbersome, bureaucratic, legalistic list of hundreds of rules and procedures. Most schools that are clearly democratic have written procedures of two to five pages. These are simple statements of what the school believes are the decisions to be made, who makes them, and how the decisions are to be finalized (see Appendix B and Appendix C).

Write It, but Not in Stone

To enact a covenant for teaching and learning, a school needs a charter for democratic decision making. Such a charter must be clearly understood, must communicate the decision-making process, and must be approved by those whom it represents.

In forming a democratic governance structure and process, the school needs to take account of the previous history of the school, the community, and the process of decision making; appropriate representation on its governing board; and the areas of schoolwide decision making that fit time schedules and the willingness of members. Once a charter is developed, it is wise to seek a trial period of at least a year, so that it can be reviewed and revised. The point is not to have a perfectly polished charter etched in stone; rather, the point is to have a guide for beginning, performing, maintaining, and building on the core work of school renewal. The major point is to begin.

Chapter Four

The Critical-Study Process: Making the Most of Important Information

I recently visited a high school that had won acclaim for its unconventional educational programs. A group of teachers, with their principal, were extolling the new work stations, the telecommunications system, and the school's technology lab. I asked them to name their school objectives. The reply was "To integrate technology into the curriculum." Thinking that they had misunderstood my question, I rephrased it: "No, what I mean is, what are you trying to accomplish for students?" The response from the principal, with enthusiastic nods of approval from her colleagues, was "To show that our school can move into the twenty-first century through technology." With a nagging feeing of disbelief, and having to move on, I dropped that line of questioning for the moment. For the next two weeks, I had the opportunity to visit and work with teams from twenty other schools, and I asked faculty from these enthusiastic elementary, middle, and high schools of their instructional objectives. The following is a list of some of their responses:

- Implement whole-language instruction in every classroom
- Use cooperative learning
- Implement interdisciplinary team teaching
- Create a literature-based critical-thinking program
- Restructure into heterogeneous, mainstreamed groupings
- Develop portfolios and performance assessments
- Assess learning styles

From their responses, which I believe typical of most "with it" schools, I realized that they were defining schoolwide instructional priorities and objectives as innovations. When I asked them how they would determine progress and achievement, their responses reaffirmed my gnawing unrest. They replied that they would determine success by whether they had learned to use the particular innovations. There is one of the great difficulties in educational renewal: the tendency to view school goals and objectives as innovations to be implemented.

To be candid, what difference does it make if a school is implementing an innovation? What should concern a school is the effects or results for students. Innovations are simply activities used as means for educating students. If a school has chosen to use an innovation, it should not be simply because people think it is "neat," "hot," or "progressive." Rather, an innovation should be chosen because it fills a need for students to learn something that is not currently being addressed (see Table 4.1). Please examine this chart.

Table 4.1. Innovations and Objectives.

Innovation	Objective
Technology	Students will learn how to use various forms of technology to improve their performance.
Cooperative learning	Students will learn how to operate in groups, and their achievement and attitudes will reflect the skills learned.
Whole-language instruction	Students will acquire a more positive attitude toward reading, read with more comprehension, and write more creatively and analytically.
Interdisciplinary instruction	Students will be better able to solve problems by drawing from the various disciplines.

A school may have different objectives in mind for a particular innovation, but what is important is that the school move away from innovations for their own sake and focus instead on the learning that is valued for students. Innovations will come and go, as they should, but educational goals and objectives for students that are derived from the covenant will endure, as they should. The litmus test for a good school is not its innovations but rather the solid, purposeful, enduring results it tries to obtain for its students. Innovations are flashy and expedient. Purposes and objectives are solid and permanent. For a school to capture the sense of school renewal, it needs to develop the critical-study process, so that information infuses the raising and studying of important questions about student learning.

Raising Questions from Within: Action Research

How does a school know where to focus resources, time, and human energy? In effect, what does it know about the results of its current educational program? When people say that they work at a good school, what do they mean? Does it feel nice? Are people happy? Are all students achieving? Is the community involved? Are students succeeding in their later schooling?

As a quick check on how conscious people are in a local school about the school's current effectiveness, one might first ask faculty and administrators and, later, parents, students, and central office officials this simple question: "What do you know about the results of the current educational programs for students?" If the respondents stare in disbelief or confusion, then one might use the following prompt: "Just tell me what you know about how the school is doing for students." Listen carefully to the responses. Do people recite platitudes? ("It is a caring place.") Do they cite statistics? ("Attendance is at 95 percent, and course grades and promotions are higher than ever before.") Do they refer to recognition? ("Our students won the district science fair.") Do they respond in terms of the results in individual classrooms, grades, or departments? Or do they simply not know how to answer, responding with generalities. Do different people give consistent information about the effectiveness of the school, or do individuals have different responses? If people can cite results, where do the results come from? Do they come from evaluations generated at the school, or from evaluations generated through assessments conducted at the district, state, or regional levels?

Such simple questioning probes for clear indicators: What data or information about effectiveness are currently collected? How complete are the data? Where are the data derived from? How do the data tap the educational purposes of the school? How does the school community share the data and use them for setting priorities and determining actions? For a school to be purposeful, all the members of its community should be seeing the big picture of how it is doing. The school should use its covenant—the principles of teaching and learning—as its boundaries. It should use its charter—the constitution for governing—as its vehicle for decision making. It should devise a critical-study process, a way of setting priorities for future actions on the basis of self-study. Information must infuse the school, so that critical thinking, generating, consuming, and action become the norms of the organization.

Data Sources for Self-Studying

The core goal of education is the preparation of students to become productive citizens in a democracy. The subgoals or objectives that come from the primary goal concern the values, skills, knowledge, and attitudes that a student needs in order to engage in the discussion and resolution of individual and social issues. What data might a school gather to inform such a preeminent goal? Some examples of data used by schools can be found in Table 4.2.[1] In reading the table, no value judgment should be applied to the worth of any particular data source. Data are classified according to *conventional sources,* from which data are readily available in virtually every school without the need for much (if any) extra time; *additional sources,* from which data can be collected with some extra effort; and *creative sources,* which usually must be developed first and require a major effort to use.

In every school there are reports, files, or accounts compiled by the school, district, or state, which give the school a standardized picture of itself. Such conventional schoolwide data probably include records of attendance; dropout rates, or student movement into and out of school; course progress reports

Table 4.2. Data Sources.

Conventional	Additional	Creative
Attendance rates	Written surveys of students, faculty, parents, community	Student exhibits
Dropout rates	Oral interviews	Student portfolios
Course progress/grades	School materials used outside school (library books, application materials)	Videotapes
Retention rates	Books read, essays written	Performance assessment
Referrals for discipline	Writing samples	
Test scores	Observations of student work in action ("shadow" studies)	
Number/percentages of students in special programs	Student progress beyond school	

or grades; failure rates; student retention rates; student refer-
rals for disciplinary action; test scores on district, state, or com-
mercially published standardized tests; and the number and percentages of students in special programs (advanced placement,
learning-disabled or remedial education, gifted-student programs). The compiling of conventional data in a form that allows them to be distributed, reviewed, and discussed by the
school community may itself raise areas of concern to be pursued. A school concerned about the democratic education of
everyone needs to raise certain issues: Why is there a dispropor-
tionate number of students of one gender or a particular ethnic
or racial group in certain classes? Why are students at a particular grade level who are taking certain subjects failing more than
others? Why are special programs enrolling more students? Why
is the socioeconomic achievement gap getting wider?

Additional data sources that a few schools may already
have, but that most could easily acquire, include the following:

- Attitude surveys of students, faculty, parents, and other community members
- Oral interviews of a random sample of students, asking about particular aspects of educational experiences in school
- Collating of school materials and activities used by students in activities outside school (leisure time, books read, letters written, diaries kept, models built, community forums participated in)
- Samples of students' writings over time
- Observations of students' work and activity during a school day, made by following ("shadowing") a small number of students and recording what they do
- Information on progress of students' work at the next grade level, determined through the gathering of follow-up reports by students, teachers (and, later, by employers)

Additional data sources can be derived by piquing the curiosity of a school community with the question "What else would we like to know about the results of our programs on students?" One highly recognized secondary school — with extremely positive community support, a 90 percent success rate of students going on to college, and excellent student performance in interscholastic competitions — decided to conduct brief interviews with twenty-five students, to find out what they had learned in school that they used outside of school. Students from a civics class designed the survey, randomly sampled the students, conducted the interviews, and analyzed the results. To the dismay of the school community, the summary indicated that students could not readily identify what they used from their school experiences. The governing body commissioned the civics class to conduct a follow-up study, to find out why students stayed in school if they saw no link between school learning and out-of-school experiences (the school had a 99 percent retention rate). The summarized result of the new study was that students remained in school to get good grades in order to go on to college, and to spend time with friends. After much discussion of the results, the governing body identified a new school-wide objective: "Students will be able to apply in-school learning

to their immediate lives outside school." A task force was formed
to look at changes in the curriculum and in staff development,
so that courses and teaching would focus more on everyday applications. The first round of data collected by the civics class
became baseline information for the launching of a schoolwide
initiative.

Creative sources of data are not yet routinely developed
and used. Examples would include student exhibits (physical
products and projects, portfolios), samples of students' ongoing work (in writing, science, mathematics, art, design, or video),
filming of a student's performance, actual work in progress, interviews, simulation exercises, activities that simulate real-life
activities (observing a student's response to reading the morn-
ing newspaper and analyzing the lead story, to filling out a job
application, to being asked about the ethical reaction to seeing
a robbery), and assessment activities (asking students to respond
to a specific challenge, such as developing an interdisciplinary
performance that includes a physical product, an oral presentation, and a written, visual, or dramatized explanation of how
the project came to its culmination).

Creative sources need carefully developed criteria for judg-
ing the competencies being demonstrated. It is a powerful learning experience for school members to engage in the creative work
of designing data sources that go beyond conventional and additional sources and use more accurate measures for assessing
the learning they are striving to promote. Some thoughtful questions have emerged from schools using creative sources: Why
are only a few students comfortable presenting in front of others?
Why do most students do well on critical thinking about a nar-
rative but poorly on spelling and grammatical skills? Why can
most students reason ethically in a simulation that concerns individual responsibilities in regard to robbery, while their actual behavior in school is accepting of theft?

An American Tendency: Action Without Study

Do not act unless you can study what you act. It is irresponsi-
ble for a school to mobilize, initiate, and act without any con-

scious way of determining whether such expenditure of time and energy is having a desirable effect. This sounds obvious, but most schools move from innovation to innovation, expending great amounts of time developing new curricula, learning new practices, and acquiring new materials and equipment. Then, after the initial enthusiasm has passed, they have no sense of whether these efforts helped students. This is the American tendency in regard to education: grab the latest innovation, get on with it as quickly as possible, and drop it just as quickly when a newer innovation appears.

To counter this American tendency, schools need to direct their attention to study as a part of their activity and not something that other people do to us. Studying a school is part of taking action in that school. To study without acting gets a school nowhere; to act without study gets a school somewhere — lost. Studying and acting, when integrated, lead to the same result — an educative, purposeful school.

Some caveats for the critical-study process of a school may prove useful:

1. Begin by looking at existing data, and decide what other data are needed.
2. Do not hesitate to act, but, when acting, figure out how to study the action.
3. Whenever possible, use existing resources within the school, district, and community to collect, analyze, and interpret data, and use students as producers of knowledge.
4. Keep the critical-study process consistent with other agencies' requirements for school improvement.

For many schools, the first step is to make everyone aware of the conventional school data, and of what those data convey before deciding whether there is a need to collect additional data. A school should use an action-oriented study: nothing kills enthusiasm and confidence more than endless study and analysis without concrete action. Most people want to get on with things, even if that means not doing a thorough study. That is fine. Get on with it, and make instructional changes; but, while doing so, figure out a way to study the effects of the change on students. At the minimum, the study should inform the school about what students are currently doing or not doing in the area of targeted action, and about what data must be collected later in order to see whether actions are having the desired results.

In collecting, analyzing, and interpreting data, identify resources within the school and the district before looking elsewhere. Are there people in the school or the district who already have data that can be summarized and given back to the school? Are there teachers pursuing graduate degrees who could conduct or collaborate in a school study that would also meet their degree requirements? Are there parents or community members who could conduct or collaborate on school studies? (A school in the West uses community volunteers to assess student performance. The community assessors compile a report on the learning strengths and weaknesses of the graduating class.) To coordinate the school's action research, are there ways of building release time or incentives in to the job description of an individual with research skills? Are there people in the district or in a nearby university or college who might have students or faculty who, upon invitation, would enjoy studying an actual school?

Most important, do not overlook students as sources for studying the school. It is tremendously valuable, as well as consistent with the primary goal of public education, for students to be involved in a study of how to improve their own community. Rather than working on contrived classroom problems of statistics, surveys, demographics, science, sociology, and psychology, it is more useful to engage students in real science, statistics, and surveys by asking them to be knowledge producers in their community. Indeed, they may meet many of the learning objectives of the school by doing such work.

Do not duplicate the critical-study process with other types of external requests for action planning. If a school is required to submit a school improvement plan as part of state or district policies, then the data collected, the priorities set, and the actions taken can be the same as for the critical study. Likewise, if a school goes through a regional accreditation process, then the data-collection plan for accreditation can be used for internal school renewal. In other words, use the covenant of teaching and learning, the charter for governance, and the critical-study process to tie most, if not all, school planning together.[2]

A generic structure for school planning usually includes the criteria found in Exhibit 4.1. Section 4, "evaluation of student results (outcomes)," is the critical-study process or component. It asks for details about baseline data collected, ongoing data collection, and information on how data will be analyzed and interpreted and how results will be used to inform further student objectives (Section 2) and revisions or changes in school activities (Section 3). Incidentally, the simultaneous use of a critical-study process along with democratic governance in a school assumes that the local school has some degree of flexibility in deriving and setting priorities for objectives, determining the most credible, useful, and compatible data, and choosing activities. If all school data, goals, objectives, activities, and results are determined and imposed by authorities outside the school, then the reader can hand this book to those authorities, suggest that they read Chapter Eight (on district and state policies), and begin a joint school-district study group on how best to renew education in an enduring manner. In the meantime, the school should look for "wiggle room" within district or state policies, so that it can find an area of need and take discretionary action, flexing previously unused muscles and seeing what can be accomplished before actual policy changes take place.

Exhibit 4.1. Generic School Plan.

Section 1.   Goal(s)

Section 2.   Student objectives

Section 3.   Activities to accomplish objectives

Section 4.   Evaluation of student results (outcomes)

Section 5.   Resources needed

(It is useful for plans to be specific in detailing *who* will be responsible for *what, when*).

Infusion of Outside Information

The critical-study process is the way in which a school assesses needs for students, plans and implements actions, and assesses results. It is, in effect, the way for a school to gather information from within. Just as important, however, is the information gathered from outside the current knowledge base of school community participants. To make decisions about important internal educational matters, without outside information about what other schools have done, what research has been compiled about similar initiatives, and what others with expertise in the matter have to say, is to limit the potential to make wise and positive decisions. A democracy is fueled by information, differing points of view, and critical reflection about varying perceptions and competing consequences. A school, as the institute given responsibility for preparing students for a democracy, should have its own decisions fueled by outside information. It is unwise to make a curriculum change, implement a staff development program, or change teaching schedules and student grouping patterns solely on the basis of what the school community currently knows. (If members act only on what they know now, the changes may be very close to what existed before). Instead, a school community needs to seek outside information and infuse it into discussions before final decisions are made. There are a number of ways to do this, including the use of professional journals, visits to other schools, conferences, graduate and university courses, invited experts (mostly practitioners from other schools), visitors, discussion groups across schools, and books, videos, and tapes.

The phrase *information age* is a cliché, but it is true that there is more information coming out daily, on virtually any topic, than any one person can digest. To keep up with current information would be more than a full-time job. That is why the retrieval of selective, important information must be built in to the decisions and operations of a school community. Each member needs to be responsible for bringing pieces of information back to the larger group. There is a wealth of knowledge about school-based education. The American Educational Research Association has an annual conference, where literally thousands of research papers are presented. There are more than twenty popular educational journals, publishing hundreds of articles monthly. Hundreds of books on education are published every year, along with thousands of audiocassettes and videos. The point is that very little of this information gets into the discussion as most public schools deliberate about change. Instead, most school debates (about such issues such as heterogeneous versus homogeneous grouping, different forms of discipline, mastery learning, transition classrooms, nongraded units, and authentic assessment) are reduced to what some people like versus what other people like. Values and feelings cannot be dismissed, nor should they be; but discussions should be filled with additional knowledge.

In this decade, it seems incongruous that so little outside information is used in schools. People are busy, information is not tailored or packaged to address specific school concerns, and schools and districts do not have systematic plans for accessing and retrieving information. Most information acquisition is a matter of chance: a course that a teacher took, a reading that someone came across, a casual conversation that someone had with a teacher from another school, a speech that someone happened to hear. To compound the problems, most of the information that school people pick up is in the context of their individual roles, not in the context of the entire school. School board members pick up information about school board matters. History teachers pick up information about the latest developments in history education. Primary-grade teachers pick up the latest techniques in their area. Principals acquire information about leadership and supervision skills. Virtually no one is acquiring information beyond his or her own field. Regardless of individual position, information about change simply is not acquired.[3] Knowledge is a form of power, and knowledge about renewing education must be commonly possessed and shared in schools. As one principal of a renewing school says, "Our job is to access the information possessed by each individual member of our school community and put all of it into our school's chest. We then have the total wealth of our community to draw on."

Outside knowledge must be sought on the basis of the school's internal study. In other words, instructional priorities, objectives, and initiatives should not be selected from a smorgasbord of highly publicized, "hot" innovations. Going shopping for a "wowser" innovation, no matter how wonderful and exciting it looks, and then making up objectives to conform with the innovation is antithetical to school renewal. The essence of school renewal is the internal, critical process of studying one's own school—looking at one's covenant, raising critical questions about current educational practice, and then assessing where the greatest priorities abide in preparing students to become productive citizens of a democracy. If a school finds that students do not exercise voice or choice in their learning, then the school goes seeking information. If the school finds that students lack respect for cultures different from their own, then the school likewise seeks information. If students are found to be less independent and self-reliant than desired, then the school seeks information. If a study finds that a group of students is falling farther behind the mainstream, then the school must seek information. If the data suggest that students need to make more productive lives for themselves in the outside world of family and home, then the school goes seeking information. To seek information means to make careful assignments in discovering the studies, readings, operations, and materials that will help the school understand more fully what can be done to address students' needs.

Ways to Gather Outside Information

Information for addressing the targeted needs of a school can be gathered in multiple ways. One or two articles in journals that synthesize research, or a few articles describing case studies of schools that have made changes, can be found and disseminated. Other schools in comparable communities, which have taken action with successful results in the targeted area, can be located and visits can be arranged. While visiting, it is helpful for a school's representatives to have a set of questions, to make sure that the most pertinent information for their own school deliberations has been gathered. School representatives can be sent to conferences where presentations are made by other school practitioners, education researchers, or theorists. Again, a format by which the information will be gathered and summarized for the school may prove useful. Members of the school community who are pursuing graduate degrees can be encouraged to take courses or seminars on the school's identified needs. Professional associations and commercial publishers have updated video- and audiotapes on current educational topics, which can be rented or purchased and shown to the school community. Well-written books on current educational topics can be assigned to school community members who will take responsibility for reading and summarizing for the group. One can find books that synthesize such areas as new learning assessments, "restructuring" programs for secondary schools, successful interventions for at-risk students, nongraded schools, interdisciplinary curricula, and multicultural education. Furthermore, the *technology* exists to keep schools informed of research and practice via television and electronic networks. There are work stations that people can use to call up, view, and hear teaching and curriculum strategies and search data bases for pertinent research.

Credible experts, preferably practitioners from schools conducting the actual work being considered, can be invited to explain procedures, discuss difficulties and successes, and give advice. The school can also actively recruit and invite visitors from other schools, who should visit with the agreement that they must "debrief" with representatives of the school community and share their knowledge of their own school operations. Another idea is to arrange periodic meetings with other schools involved in school renewal and share questions, practices, and results. This is easily done within districts. Teams of four to seven representatives from individual schools can meet every month or every quarter. On a larger scale, schools across districts can have meetings sponsored by regional, state, university, or professional associations.

Building Professional Craft Knowledge

In discussing information infusion and sources of knowledge, there is the risk of sounding condescending and of stating the

obvious to people who work in organizations where information infusion is a natural part of doing business. Nevertheless,
in my experience, I am often saddened by the isolation of schools
from outside information. What appears so obvious — the need
for information — has little formal support in or from school districts and stage agencies. Instead, many schools that seek information must rely on individual members to find time in their
busy lives and figure out how to get it. Professional libraries
in schools are not well stocked. Systematic visits are not provided
to other schools. Gaining information from visitors is not planned. Large sums of money are spent, either to send one or two
people to an expensive state or national conference, where no
helpful information comes back to the schools, or to pay the high
cost of a consultant who conducts a workshop. Money would
be much better spent on travel expenses for school community
members to visit other schools engaged in the real work of educational renewal. The strength of information carried back and
forth between credible and purposeful practitioners is largely
ignored.

Most schools do not know what is going on in other schools
as close as a few blocks away, nor do they know about exemplary practices in full implementation throughout regions, states,
and the nation. The legitimacy of practice is diminished when
knowledge is purchased and its sources are fed mainly by the
consulting, research, and writing of people who are far removed
from the day-to-day practices of a school.

Giving Voice

One elementary school suggests the voluntary selection of a "book
of the summer" and begins its fall term with discussions about
what that book has to say about planning for improving the curriculum. A middle school commissions a task force of volunteers to be a study or action research group for one year, to deal
with the objective of students' using multiple modes of learning. The task force is given a budget to track down articles, read
books, attend conferences, and report on findings, recommendations of schoolwide actions, and suggested data-collection

procedures. An urban high school establishes a group of students, teachers, parents, and community members to visit exemplary dropout-prevention secondary programs in other urban schools and recommend changes in their own school. Every member of a school community who is given the time, the money, or the opportunity to become informed about an identified educational priority has an obligation to report the information obtained. There have been countless instances when individuals learned on school time, or with school money, information that was of use only to themselves. Another benefit of using school community members to report outside information is that this process gives voice to previously voiceless people.

In every school, there are some people who constantly add their opinions to school discussions in a loud, dominating manner. These people have a clear voice in school issues, but they often add little knowledge. There are other members of school communities who typically relinquish their voices to more aggressive members. Either they feel that they have little to offer, or they are timid and afraid of consequences. Lambs can become lions when given an opportunity to acquire information that others do not possess. Suddenly (and it has been sudden and dramatic), quiet and passive Mr. Garcia is seen and heard forcefully informing loud and opinionated Ms. Anderson, "It is not true that we cannot change this. I just visited King School, and their community is more traditional than ours, but they have been operating this way for three years. It can be done — I have seen it!"

Specialized knowledge gives volume to those without voice. It can lower the volume of those with dominating voices. Most important, it provides an expanded information base for the entire school.

Part Two

The Work
of School Renewal

Chapter Five

Educational Tasks
and Organizational Readiness

The three-dimensional framework for supporting school renewal is illustrated in Figure 5.1. The *covenant* — principles of learning — gives the school a consistency of educational purpose. The *charter,* in the form of a constitution, provides the governance vehicle for democratic, schoolwide educational decisions. The *critical-study process* provides a systematic way for collecting and analyzing student data in order to set learning priorities

Figure 5.1. School Renewal Framework.

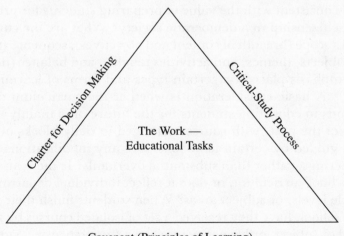

Covenant (Principles of Learning)

and infuse the school with information. The work of a self-renewing school exists within the three-dimensional framework. Now it is time to focus on that work, to serve the ultimate goal of education: preparing students to become productive citizens of our democracy. The educational tasks of a school are curriculum development, staff development, coaching work, instructional program development, student assessment, and instructional budget management.

The following are simple descriptions and questions to be asked for each task and the way the task is directly related to how teachers teach, what students learn, and how the school narrows the gap between current practice and its covenant for teaching and learning. When work on these tasks is not the substance of a school's governance, power for students is lost, and the school becomes, at best, a more congenial (but not collegial) place for adults. For our purposes here, the tasks are treated as mutually exclusive, but this is not the case in practice.

Curriculum

The curriculum is the program of study for students. Does the existing curriculum correspond to how students learn and to what they should learn? How was the curriculum developed in the past? Is it consistent with the value of preparing students for productive citizenship in a democratic society? What are the curriculum's scope (breadth of content and objectives), sequence (order of subjects, themes, and activities taught), and balance (degree of emphasis placed on certain types and forms of learning)?

A basic consideration is whether the curriculum corresponds to educating students for the future or is mainly a vestige of the past, with courses arranged in daily blocks of time and guided by certain textbooks. Are any modifications mere tinkerings, rather than substantial overhauls? Is there an overall school curriculum, or does it reflect individual departments, grade levels, or subject areas? When students finish their years in a school, have they received a set of isolated courses by grade level or subject, or have they received a comprehensive, cumulative educational program that prepares them to be critical, self-reliant, and confident people in dealing with matters of personal life and society? For example, are social and community issues built in to disciplines and subjects across the curriculum? Are issues of multicultural education integrated into the curriculum, or do they appear only in special events or celebrations? Does the curriculum reflect the concerns and values of the community, and do parents and community members have a chance to be involved? Does what students learn have real applications? Does it involve them in applications to life outside of school? Does learning serve the larger community? Do students have an active, ongoing voice in what they learn?

Another set of inquiries has to do with how the curriculum is developed. Does the existing curriculum come from the ideas, thoughts, and work of the local faculty and school community, or is it determined by others at the district or state levels? How prescriptive is the curriculum? Is it controlled and monitored by the use of particular textbooks, tests, and workbooks, or is there flexibility for faculty to adopt their own sequencing and materials? Finally, how does a school decide whether the curriculum should be left alone, modified and revised, or thrown out and redone entirely?

Staff Development

The formally stipulated, paid, or required activities provided to upgrade the staff's knowledge and skills are what is meant by the term *staff development*. School-based staff development activities may involve early-release days; preplanning, planning, and postplanning days built in to the contracted year; professional days for attending meetings, workshops, and conferences; stipends or certification credit for taking classes, workshops, or courses; and time at faculty meetings devoted to learning activities. Staff development is defined here as not including educational activities pursued by educators on their own time and at their own expense (graduate programs, attendance at their own professional associations' meetings, educational trips to other countries).

What does the faculty need to learn in order to improve, refine, or embellish its teaching practices across the entire school and become more consistent with the covenant for teaching and learning? Should a school ensure that all students in all classrooms have teachers who use a variety of teaching techniques, so that no one method (such as lecturing or seatwork) dominates? Should a school ensure that all teachers learn how to make more intensive use of technology in the classroom, or should the student's experiences with technology depend on the teacher to whom the student is assigned? Should a school have faculty members who have learned to use positive, mediating discipline techniques? Should teachers know how to use mastery learning techniques, cooperative learning, critical-thinking strategies, constructivist approaches, or project- and community-centered learning activities?

Another series of questions has to do with the use of staff development in the school. Do most individuals develop their own staff development plans? Does the district provide most of the staff development workshops and courses? What percentage of time and money for staff development goes toward schoolwide activities consistent with the learning goals and objectives of the school?

Coaching

Coaching has to do with the amount and type of personal feedback and consultation, derived from firsthand observation, that teachers receive on their teaching. With no feedback or discussion from others, it is difficult for an individual teacher to know how consistent his or her teaching is with the school covenant, or how to become more consistent with it. Leaving people alone to do the best they can sends a quiet but clear message: the school is not really serious about teachers' learning from one another and becoming a school community; privacy is more important. Coaching does not involve employee evaluation and compliance; rather, it involves a formative process, provided to each person in the organization, to help the school strengthen teaching and learning.

How often do teachers have people (administrators and other teachers) come into their classrooms for extended periods to observe the principles of learning that the teachers are striving to implement? Does such observation include discussion, to help guide teachers' further planning? How aware are teachers of one another's teaching? Is there a system for releasing faculty to visit with one another and focus on particular schoolwide teaching purposes? Are such visits reciprocal and collaborative, rather than remedial and hierarchical (peer coaching relationships, rather than mentor-mentee or master teacher–lead teacher relationships)? How clearly is it understood that these visits, observations, and discussions, regardless of who initiates them, are for purposes of assistance, rather than for ranking and evaluation?

More refined questions about coaching have to do with who visits whom. For a school to be a community, its members need to be aware of the entire school. Peer coaching that goes on primarily within grade levels, teams, or departments reinforces the idea that the school is mainly a physical space for the particular groups. Instead, faculty need to spend time observing and discussing teaching with teachers at other grade levels, in other departments, on other teams, and in other physical places within the school. This arrangement gives each faculty member a better sense of the entire school. There can also be a role for parents and community members to assist a school in its coaching process, and students can visit other classrooms to find connections across seemingly disparate grade levels and courses.

Instructional Programs

By contrast with curriculum and staff development tasks, instructional programs are externally constructed, field-tested, and occasionally validated packages of materials, teaching techniques, and assessments, which are learned and implemented. To name a few, there now exist effective school programs, peer coaching programs, cooperative learning programs, master teaching programs, assertive discipline programs, whole-language programs, dropout-prevention programs, interdisciplinary programs, critical-thinking programs, and computer teaching programs. Many such programs are simplistic, commercial, and marketed with the idea that local practitioners cannot figure out what to do for themselves. Nevertheless, there are some carefully constructed programs that can be helpful to a school when it knows what to do, and buying into such programs can be a way to begin addressing school learning priorities.

Some hard questions must be asked about any instructional program being contemplated or being used in a school. How did it come to exist? Who decided on it? Who judged that it was worth the time and money? Most important, how does it fit into the larger goals and priorities of the school? In other words, what is such a program supposed to accomplish, and how is it compatible with the schoolwide covenant? What research can inform the school about whether such a program is worth continuing or revising?

Another set of questions has to do with a program that has not yet been acquired. Before the purchase of books, manuals, training programs, and equipment, are other options being thoroughly explored? Can the same time and money for the program (even if it is compatible with the school's covenant and priorities) be used by the school to develop its own program and thus ensure greater commitment and local expertise? If not, has the school checked out the claims of the program, visiting schools that have been using it for at least several years?

Student Assessment

The various ways of assessing student learning must also be examined in order to improve teaching and learning in a school. A truism in education is that teachers teach what students are tested on. Schools that believe standardized tests are the best measures of student learning arrange their classrooms and use instructional time and teaching techniques differently from the schools that believe students' actual performance is the more important measure of learning. In the former case, classrooms are organized for students to learn sequences of skills and knowledge in a more directive, teacher-centered manner. In the latter case, students have more open-ended opportunities in classroom activities and discussions.

Schools need to take a close look at how they assess individual students, how they use such individual assessments, and how they report such assessment to students and parents, since assessment is a powerful influence on teaching. The school community's very involvement in deciding about assessment devices changes teaching. The high school that requires a year-long performance exhibition that integrates communication, physical representation, and a written scientific rationale as a graduation requirement now forces the curriculum, instructional programs, and staff development across departments to be more reflective of such integrative assessment.

Are the school's current testing and assessment practices consistent with the covenant? Are there glaring gaps between what the school claims to believe about learning and what it assesses? Is how student learning is recorded (report cards, progress reports) consistent with the covenant? Are the results of student learning assessments used constructively to guide future planning of work among faculty members, students, and the rest of the community? How can parents, other community members, and students become more involved in the development and implementation of new assessment procedures and reports?

Assessment has emerged recently as a crucial issue in public education and in the confidence that a community has in its schools. This issue, as well as most others in this book, will not be resolved overnight and will have to be worked on one step at a time. What is most auspicious in this new questioning of traditional assessment practices is that schools, through a democratic governance process, may have the opportunity to develop, within their communities, measures of the greatest worth that are consistent with their agreed-upon covenants. Thus they will be able to demonstrate that the learning of greatest worth is being achieved.

The Instructional Budget

Very few people or organizations have the money that they desire or need, but the existing money can still be a resource in a school that has control over the budget and pays for staff positions, teaching materials, and staff development time. Traditionally, most of the instructional budget has been used to support normal school operations. Each year, the same amounts are spent in basically the same ways, to do the same things (replacing teachers, adopting new textbooks and testing forms and scoring services, and setting aside planning days). With more money, a school can surely do more for its students, but the first two pragmatic questions are "With our existing money, are we doing the right thing? With more money, would we be doing more of the right things?"

Is the current instructional budget being used to fuel the school covenant and the school priorities, rather than being divided among various "fiefdoms" within the school and going where it has always gone? Why spend money on textbooks, if other learning materials are more relevant to the learning principles? Why divide resources by department and grade level, if the school is striving for schoolwide goals? Information is power. Money is power, too. By seeing the total instructional budget not as having to be spent as in the past but as a flexible resource to use for school priorities, the school community gains additional power.[1]

Money is a sensitive issue for many district officials and school administrators, who want to "play" the budget "close to the vest" so as to have room to respond to special needs or emergencies. But democracies that work well keep their funds in the open and decide collectively on the best uses. In societies where individuals keep public funds hidden, personal cults of dependency and blind trust are cultivated, and the potential for abuse and unethical conduct is created. Such abuse of confidence, intentional or not, can be read about every day in the newspapers. Local schools do not need to keep faculty and staff members or other community members ignorant when it comes to how funds are spent. If a democracy is real, then part of its reality is its resources. For the school to decide what it wants for students is the first step. The second step is to allocate its resources accordingly.

Implementing New Practices

It is one thing to know about all these tasks. It is another to decide on appropriate implementation. For more than a decade, research on educational innovations, whatever their nature, has shown that what a school community learns and sustains, in terms of new ways of teaching and new ways of student learning, follows a rather commonsensical three-phase sequence.[2]

First, new approaches to teaching and learning must be explained and then demonstrated. The faculty needs to understand what the approach is about, what it purports to do, what it consists of, and what the results have been. It is then necessary to see what it looks like, how the materials are used, what teaching methods are employed, what technology is employed, how students are organized, and how classrooms are to be physically arranged.

Second, the faculty needs opportunities for role playing, applied practice, and feedback. Once the faculty sees how the approach works, the internalization process begins. Teachers use the new approaches with other teachers in workshops, under the guidance of a person with expertise in those approaches. At the next level, faculty members move to their own classrooms and practice the new approaches with students on a trial basis, for a set duration. During this piloting phase, skills are sharpened if colleagues who also are piloting the change observe and give nonjudgmental feedback to one another.

Third, implementation is sustained by having faculty members involved in ongoing meetings, where they share, brainstorm, and revise the use of the new approaches. Once teachers have piloted the new approaches and received feedback from colleagues or experts, they will be more likely to change their previous routines and adopt the new approaches. Implementation will be maintained if the faculty has continual opportunities to discuss and share successes, failures, and ongoing concerns. In such settings, colleagues help refine one another's skills, find new adaptations, and keep the focus on change until the change becomes a normal operation within the school.

It is important to note that participants need to be involved and to see an innovation as part of their school's overall direction. According to participants' concerns, there may be a need to give greater emphasis to a particular phase of this three-stage sequence. It takes extended practice and application before a particular change becomes routinized. After that, however, conceptual distinctions among previous educational tasks disappear in long-term implementation of new schoolwide approaches to teaching and learning.

Stages of Concern

Ideas for change in teaching approaches should come from the people who will be affected. Approaches must be developed from the covenant and the charter, so that the activities will express a mandate from those who govern themselves. Therefore, the old problem of resistance to externally imposed ideas about school reform should become less of an issue. The larger issue becomes one of degree of emphasis and pacing of change. Those who have studied the change literature have noted that the demise of many reforms has been due to a failure to account for the specific stages of participants' concerns.[3]

Here, we will consider three stages of concern: *orientation, integration,* and *refinement.* These stages are illuminated by the major questions that participants have about particular instructional changes.

The orientation phase is guided by the central question "Why should I do this?" The integration phase is guided by the question "How do I integrate the approach into my classroom?" The refinement phase is guided by the question "How can I do better what I already do?"

Suppose that a school community has determined, in accord with its covenant, and after having collected data on student needs, that a high priority is for every student to be able to use advanced technologies as a learning tool in all areas of the curriculum. A task force recommends a three-year plan to reeducate all faculty, identify technology resources in the community, find students who can be technical assistants to teachers, and reallocate instructional funds to develop a technology studio and center in the school. The plan is approved.

Some faculty members are technophobic. They know that advanced technologies are around them in their daily lives, but they do not yet have computers in their own homes. They teach subjects that traditionally have relied on books, paper, and pencils. They say, "I know that this technology is good, and I agreed to it as a school priority, but why should I learn how to use such technology in my classroom? How will it improve my students' learning, and how will it improve my life as an educator?" These are concerns of orientation.

Other faculty members are perhaps less phobic about technology and do not resist its increased use. They just have not taken the time to upgrade their own skills. They say, "I know that this is for the twenty-first century, but I am still in the twentieth century. Anyway, let's get on with it. Show me how all this stuff works and how I should use it with my kids." Their concerns are with integration.

Finally, there are technology hogs, who for years have sequestered most of the school's computers for their own students. They constantly bring in their own technology from home. They go to workshops, take courses, and subscribe to the latest magazines to keep up on developments in the field. This group is always trying to find new ways to expand students' experiences with laser disks, electronic bulletin boards, and other advances. They say, "Of course technology should be a top school priority; it should have been years ago. Now I want to take its use to a new level in my classroom and in our school. How can I go beyond what I am currently doing?" The concern here is with the betterment and refinement of current practice.

Let us stay with this illustration and return to the three phases of implementing educational change. Even if all, or nearly all, the participants have agreed to the change, their levels of concern may be different, and the implementation may fail if planning is not sensitive to this difference.

Those at the orientation stage need explanation and demonstration, so that they can understand the benefits and see how others like themselves have used the new approach in their classrooms. Those at the integration stage need more trial and practice, role playing, classroom practice, and feedback from others. Those at the refinement stage need more time for exploring and troubleshooting with other users via group brainstorming and problem solving. Mismatching stages of concern with phases of implementation may ensure failure, while matching the stages and phases can help guide the pace and emphasis of school change (see Table 5.1).

Table 5.1. Matching Implementation to Concerns.

Implementation Phase	Stage of Concern
Explanation and demonstration	Orientation
Role playing, classroom practice, and feedback	Integration
Group brainstorming and problem solving	Refinement

A school community may spend a great deal of time bringing in outsiders to explain and demonstrate an approach. If
teachers are already convinced of the need and are at the integration and refinement stages of concern, they will be bored and
will sense that the school is losing valuable time. A school may
spend an inordinate amount of time on role playing, classroom
practice, and feedback. If teachers are mostly at the orientation
stage, there is a clear risk of turning the participants off and creating hostility. To spend time showing people how to do something when they still are not sure why they should is to set the
conditions for failure. Similarly, to spend a great deal of time
on group brainstorming and problem solving with teachers who
are mainly at the orientation and integration stages is to ask people
for cutting edge expertise before they have spent enough time
piloting the approach. In these circumstances, activities become
superficial, and wasteful exercises in pooling ignorance.

Of course, teachers do not fall neatly into stages of concern, nor does implementation fall into a clean, invariable sequence of phases. In most schools, teachers have multiple levels
of concern with educational approaches. Nevertheless, these
stages and phases can give further understanding of the complexities of school change and, when accounted for, can help
give schools criteria for determining overall plans.

Once the people associacted with a school have decided
to harness their resources according to school priorities and
plans, they must work together to make the planned educational
change a reality. This does not happen when teachers are simply separated into three groups, according to level of concern,
and treated as separate entities. Educational change becomes
a reality when there is a main plan for activities in which all

teachers participate, with opportunities for small groups to do more specialized work and opportunities for individuals to receive more personal attention. A school community furthers implementation by encouraging people at different levels of proficiency and achievement to work together on common priorities. A successful school provides its faculty with a heterogeneous organization, so that all groups and individuals can accomplish the goals. Adults learn to form a more productive organization by using among themselves the same covenant, or principles of learning, that they desire for their students.

Blurring of Tasks

Educational tasks are the enabling activities that accomplish school priorities. In practice the tasks should not stand separately. This is where schools can lose energy and direction. Curriculum development should coincide with staff development. Coaching should reinforce curriculum and staff development. Instructional programs and student assessment should reflect corresponding changes in curriculum. The instructional budget should provide resources for supporting the whole. When each task is seen as a project unto itself, with its own goals, activities, and budget, a school merely has a set of "projects" going on, with no articulation of its covenant.

Many highly innovative schools have no links and do not know where they are going. In an individual school, one can find the curriculum being changed to reflect scientific literacy across disciplines, while the staff development program is some popular student discipline approach, the coaching is based on another project such as "teacher effectiveness," the assessment of student learning is being revised with a "higher order thinking" core, and the instructional budget is being doled out by the priority of whoever yells loudest. When the people are asked about overall learning goals for students and about how the various tasks may be purposefully related, the typical reaction in these innovative schools is "Well, they *must* be related, somehow."

A successful school community performs its tasks quite differently from a school that is juggling numerous discrete projects. Consider the schoolwide learning objective of a middle school: to have students understand the various forms of mass communication and know how to use media (television, radio, print advertisements, film, and newspapers) to participate in issues of the local community. Developing such an objective is relatively easy; planning to attain the objective is hard. A school attains this goal by examining its educational tasks, developing activities across tasks, and aligning its human and financial resources. Answers to these questions integrate those tasks:

1. How do we need to change our curriculum across the school to reflect this new emphasis?
2. What staff development will be essential for faculty?
3. What coaching will be necessary to give feedback to teachers in implementing the curriculum and the new teaching strategies?
4. What external instructional programs, materials, and packages would it be useful to incorporate into the changes in curriculum, staff development, and coaching?
5. What changes have to be made in how we assess student learning, to determine the progress made on this objective?
6. How much money and time should we allocate, and what resources from the community can we secure, for attainment of this objective?

Departmental and Grade-Level Plans

Not every learning objective needs an individual plan. If a school has many learning objectives, a plan that shows how they all can be accomplished is appropriate. Furthermore, a school needs to avoid spending so much time on planning that it never gets around to taking action. Action, planning, and study should be simultaneous; one activity should feed information into the others.

Schoolwide emphasis may sound fine, but aren't there different groups, with their own alignments and distinct purposes? Will they surrender their purposes to the common good? In the ordinary world of schools, the focus is on subgroups. In high schools, departments stick together and have their own budgets and planning meetings. In the middle school, departmental or, more often, grade-level teams and specialists work together. In the elementary school, grade- and age-level groups work together. Nothing in our discussion so far contradicts the reality that subgroups do work together to attain schoolwide goals. The individual subgroups of a school, as long as the school is organized that way, will continue to have some of their own curricula, staff development, coaching, instructional programs, assessment, and instructional budgets. But subgroups' plans can be developed as semiautonomous parts of the overarching covenant and goals. They become individual patches of the quilt. They are not the quilt itself.

Chapter Six

Becoming an Educative Community

A reader involved with her local school might muse, "This sounds nice so far. The three-dimensional framework and the educational tasks make sense. What more can there be?"

There are some more subtle considerations about internal change, power, and disequilibrium. The less obvious factors offer guidance to the school community about when and where to enter into school renewal. This chapter and the following one focus on the school. The remaining chapters address the role of the school district, the school board, the teachers' union or association, the state, and the nation in developing appropriate policies and providing support for school-level work.

Change and the Light Switch

It has been said that the average person would take two to three weeks of daily fumbling around before feeling secure in consistently finding a relocated light switch in the living room. Only after incessant trials would the new location of the switch become imprinted in his or her mind, and unconscious and sure movement to the switch become routine. School renewal is a bit more complicated than that. What is being discussed here is a community of people, mobilized to take purposeful educational action together. To accomplish such action to the point of unthinking routine, however, is probably impossible and would be largely undesirable, and simply getting to a level of ordinary comfort normally takes one to three years. The biggest obstacle is learning how to be comfortable with discomfort. Disequilibrium is the constant of school renewal.

What is characteristic of self-renewing, democratic schools is that, at any particular moment, members' experiences seem challenging, trying, and frustrating. Yet, over time, crises are defused, issues are resolved, and schools progress. In other words, a school community is never sure how immediate problems will be handled; the unexpected keeps cropping up, but a school learns to be confident that it *will* solve any immediate problem as one hurdle in a line of decisions that will continue to make the school a better place for students. Confidence comes from knowing that decisions will be derived from the covenant, the charter, and the critical-study process, so that there is an underlying reflective and moral purpose to what is done. The change process constantly knocks a school off its feet. The school learns that it cannot avoid getting knocked down, but it can learn how to get back up safely and keep on moving.

Confidence with the Unknown: Development Paths

What is a school community ready to do? What are individuals ready to do? How does a school mobilize as a community but still respect individual and group differences? To answer these questions, it is helpful to look at approaches to change and at considerations of human development.

Three approaches that are known to change people are the *authoritarian and advisory approach,* the *input-and-selection approach,* and the *collaborative approach.* Each approach is predicated on a different degree of choice and responsibility for the people affected.

In the authoritarian and advisory approach, individuals and groups are told what they have to do in order to keep their jobs. People with formal authority and control over the professional lives of others *make* them do whatever is deemed best. Individuals and group members may be asked for their input, and they may serve in advisory roles, but final decisions clearly come from power over subordinates. Decisions may be presented in a dictatorial fashion or in a benevolent and open way, but the approach is the same. Someone ultimately decides for others.

In the input-and-selection approach, individuals and groups are given a set of acceptable choices from which to select. The group members may give input into the determination of acceptable alternatives, but a person with formal authority over others decides on the final choices. That person allows group members to choose from among the options that are acceptable to the formal authority. This is power over others, with choice.

In the collaborative approach, no hierarchy of authority determines changes. People within the formal hierarchy accept the same rights and responsibilities, vote as others do, and act as others do. Decisions are made through equal distribution of power.

These approaches can be analyzed in terms of power and of responsibility for consequences. Motivation theory associates responsibility with choice: when choice is absent, so often is responsibility. In the authoritarian and advisory approach, group members have no choice; therefore, they take little responsibility for the consequences of decisions and make changes only because of the rewards or retributions involved. In the input-and-selection approach, members have a degree of choice within alternatives; to the extent that they believe in the viability of the choices, they take some responsibility for the consequences. If things go wrong, however, they can disown responsibility for the consequences. In the collaborative approach, no group member can hide from the consequences of a decision; whatever has been decided is a group decision, and the entire group is responsible. Table 6.1 depicts degrees of choice and responsibility.

Let us make some clear points about school renewal:

1. A public school, in fulfilling its highest purpose, should be democratic in decisions about the core work of schoolwide teaching and learning.
2. There are other areas of decision making—within a school, between the school and the district, and between the school and its local community—that must be negotiated in terms of control, responsibility, and consequences. The authoritarian and advisory approach, the input-and-selection ap-

Table 6.1. Choice, Responsibility, and Control.

	Authoritarian and Advisory Approach	*Input-and-Selection Approach*	*Collaborative Approach*
Degree of Choice	Low	Moderate	High
Degree of responsibility	Low	Moderate	High
Control by formal hierarchical position	Yes	Yes	No

proach, or the collaborative approach may be an appropriate approach for decision making outside the core.

3. Schools and individuals vary in their developmental readiness for fully collaborative, democratic work.

Point 1 has been addressed in previous chapters. The core, internal, and professional work of schoolwide teaching and learning should be decided by a school community via a collaborative, democratic process that includes all stakeholders and gives a major voice to faculty members. Point 2 suggests that other issues in a school need not be decided democratically and may best be left to the authoritarian and advisory approach or to the input-and-selection approach. A principal, a community group, or a special committee can be assigned the authority to make decisions, so as not to drain the time and energy of the school community away from its essential work. It is senseless to use a collaborative approach to decide all school matters, just as it is senseless not to use a collaborative, democratic approach to decide matters of educational change. Point 3 shows that not all schools are ready for full democratization of core work, and this point needs careful explanation.

Developmental Needs

There are schools that have virtually no history of their members working together. There has been little cross-departmental or cross–grade-level work, and there has been no record of faculty giving input into schoolwide decisions. Furthermore, there has been little community and student involvement, outside of perfunctory fundraising activities or social events. Basically, many schools in America operate as fiefdoms of the school principal, of a special-interest group within, or of the superintendent and board. There may be audible rumblings of discontent in these schools, or (what is most likely) school members may have resigned themselves. This does not mean that the principal, a special-interest group, or the district has consciously decided that the school should operate in this way. It may be that there is simply no awareness of another way to operate.

These are the conventional public schools. They are not going to move soon, or on their own, to collaboration and democracy in school renewal. In such schools, individuals may be extremely uncomfortable working in groups, honestly sharing ideas, and publicly confronting one another. Such practices may have incurred the wrath of authority in the past. Some individuals may also be used to dominating, overseeing discussions, and manipulating others out of the action. Others may be used to staying in the background, not speaking up, and deferring to authority. Interpersonal matters, hidden agendas, and old traditions are not going to dissipate all at once, or once and for all.

Conventional schools that have worked predominantly under an authoritarian approach need to begin involving their members in making choices within constructed boundaries: the input-and-selection approach. Schools where much work has already been done with the input-and-selection approach, whereby authorities clearly outline acceptable parameters, should begin to identify concrete, small-scope educational issues that can be collaboratively agreed upon, so that all members share equally in decisions. Schools that are already predominantly collaborative should look at how to refine, focus, and streamline existing operations into a clear democracy around core work.

One subtle consideration for school communities is individuals' current developmental levels of thinking about and commitment to schoolwide educational change. It is well documented that people with limited thinking—limited experience and knowledge—about a topic desire and need structure from authorities or experts. They view help as being told how to do something. People who do have experience in and knowledge of a particular area tend to view authorities or experts as sources of information for their own thinking, rather than as dispensers of truth. Those with little concern about a particular topic tend to want somebody else to make decisions for them: "I don't care what we do. Just tell me, so I can get on with my life." Those with considerable concern tend to want to be involved with decisions: "I care deeply about this. Before a decision is made, I want to be involved." Table 6.2 shows the relationship between developmental readiness and the appropriate approach to change.

Table 6.2. Developmental Levels of
Knowledge and Concern with School Renewal.

Thought (Knowledge and Experience)	Concern and Commitment	Appropriate Approach
Low	Low	Authoritarian and advisory
Moderate	Moderate	Input-and-selection
High	High	Collaborative

To oversimplify, for now, some quick applications of Table 6.2 can be made. A school where most members are not highly concerned or knowledgeable about school renewal will need to work initially on a more structured, smaller scale than a school where most members are highly committed and highly knowledgeable. In most schools, there is not a single clear dimension to development; individuals range over the entire continuum. Development also varies according to the topic of educational renewal. Some people are highly committed to curriculum work. Others do not care. Still others may be highly thoughtful about learning assessment but may give little thought to instructional programs.

At best, such developmental considerations boil down to estimates about the degree of thought and commitment to educational renewal. Are most people at a level that would suggest a major, multifaceted overhaul of the educational program all at once? Or are there more people who simply have little knowledge about doing anything other than what has always been done? Should more time be devoted to studying and understanding school renewal before a plan is developed? Is there a small group of knowledgeable enthusiasts who could start moving the school beyond its current ways of operating? If so, how can they cooperate with the others to get a few educational initiatives under way?

The developmental perspective is also a lens for viewing how people change as a school becomes more democratic. Do more or fewer people than expected get involved? Is more thought being exhibited about school change? Over time, does the change approach enable more people to move to higher levels of development? If people's thought and commitment are increasing or decreasing, what does that suggest about speeding up or slowing down schoolwide efforts?

Sociocultural Differences

How people respond to involvement, structure, control, and choice may also vary according to sociocultural factors. For example, what appears to be a faculty member's unwillingness to be engaged may be something else. It may be that some people feel excluded. The covenant, the charter, and the critical-study process all demand information sharing, candid communication, and serious, collaborative decision making. However, men tend to dominate discussions with women and compete with one another for center stage, often ignoring or interrupting women. Men also tend to reason according to universal rules, and they often use military and sports analogies, while women tend to reason more from a sense of human and personal caring for others and to use analogies with nurturance. Men tend to communicate with each other differently from how women communicate with each other, and when they are together they communicate with each other differently from the way they do when apart. (Such distinctions, of course, do not apply to every man and woman.) Miscommunication or lack of communication among members of a school community may be mistaken for lack of interest in the work.

Other sociocultural factors that influence communication have to do with age, socioeconomic class, and cultural or racial identity. The experiences, impressions, and idioms of one's youth and young adult life have a deep influence on one's perceptions and life-style. Adults who came of age during the Depression, World War II, the era of the civil rights struggle, the Woodstock era, and the high-tech 1980s view and express beliefs about the world differently. People who grew up in affluent communities, in middle-income neighborhoods, and in poverty also differ in outlook. The same is true for the differences in attitude and belief among those raised in rural, suburban, and city environments, as well as among those from different regions of the country.

An even more powerful definer of perceptions is one's cultural or racial group. The cultures, norms, and values of the countries from which people immigrated or were exiled, recently or not, may impart distinct characteristics of attitude and communication. For example, what appears respectful and honest in one culture — to look someone squarely in the eye, communicate simply and directly, and keep one's voice at a steady level — can be seen as disrespectful in another culture. The idea of authority and how it varies by socioeconomic factors is also intriguing. There are cultures where authority is vested in elders, women, men, secret groups, or no one. Thus many subtle dynamics may come into play when a school is trying to become a forceful community.

What to Do About Developmental and Sociocultural Differences

First, realize that people do vary. It is dangerous to assume that everyone should see the world in the same way, communicate in the same way, and have the same level of enthusiasm. Instead, a school community needs to engage in constant testing, to see how much willingness there is to develop and use the covenant, the charter, and the critical-study process. One never knows how much thought and commitment truly exist in a school until people are invited to participate.

Second, get started. Regardless of how it is assessed, the proof of developmental readiness is what happens in a school when its members are given greater choice and responsibility. Do they take it and run, or do they avoid it and hide? What communication problems crop up? What sociocultural or developmental differences are revealed? Dealing with differences become a by-product of the work itself, rather than a prelude to the work. This means that work on multicultural understanding, team building, and group dynamics cannot stand alone in preparing a school for change. Such work is done as the school develops and learns how to renew education.

Third, move to the next level of choice and responsibility. If your school has been mostly authoritarian and advisory, identify small and concrete schoolwide educational needs, and establish voluntary interest groups to make recommendations to the entire school community within preestablished parameters. If your school has operated mostly in the input-and-selection mode, establish educational areas for shared governance, with equal distribution of power. Take relatively small-scale concerns, and let the process be a minipilot for a full-scale conversion to democracy. If your school has norms of collegiality and shared decision making, renew all at once, with comprehensive activity emanating from the covenant, the constitution, and the critical-study process.

Fourth, accept that collaboration and democracy will be built and rebuilt over time. As a school aims to realize an internal model of democratic society, to prepare its students for a similar society outside the school, the need to understand the discursive nature of the work is paramount. To plan and implement educational activities is worthy, not only for what it accomplishes but also for what it does not. Both success and failure can guide future plans and activities if the areas targeted for change are selected so as to secure information for future deliberations. Therefore, the initial areas of change in a neophyte school should not be so far-reaching in magnitude and resources that the failure to implement change would cripple the school in the future.

The Need for Disequilibrium

Success is the intelligent use of mistakes in self-renewing schools. The moral imperative of the school is for its members to move into their areas of incompetence: if we already knew exactly how to do this work, we would not have the purposeless cycles of educational reform that schools are endlessly caught in. We all need to learn new roles and relationships.

It will be frightening for faculty members to share truly in the governance of their school, for principals or central office officials to give up traditional authority and power, and for students and the community to have a real voice. Everyone will have to give up some prerogatives in order to foster collective autonomy. Power given up by individuals and small groups can be power gained by the school community.

For the new order to be realized, every individual has to lose his or her secure place in the old scheme. Teachers can no longer argue solely for their own classrooms, grade levels, or departments. Principals can no longer resort to their status and authority in making decisions. Parents can no longer fight for what is best for their children alone. School boards, superintendents, and central office personnel can no longer impose uniform procedures and regulations. To make decisions in the interest of all students means to create disequilibrium. In most cases, the new order will not be comfortable.

The school will have to decide about what is the best it can do at the moment, learn from that, and carry on. Once begun, the roller-coaster ride will continue through some dramatic twists and turns.

Chapter Seven

Dealing with
Tough Questions of Practice

With the three-dimensional framework of the covenant, the charter, and the critical-study process explained, and with developmental and sociocultural factors taken into account, the real work of schools — the educational tasks of curriculum and staff development, instructional programs, coaching, and assessment — can be planned and implemented. The routine, surface quiet of the school is now broken, as it should be if school community members are knowingly stepping into uncharted waters and changing the security of people's positions, roles, and responsibilities.

The results of research on organizations show that the most successful communities experience the greatest conflict in their original decisions about change. Public conflict indicates that an issue is important, that people see themselves as having a real influence on decisions, and that information about possible options and consequences is multiplying. The absence of public conflict in school change can be a danger sign. It can indicate that people do not care, do not believe that there is any merit in making their views known, and prefer to go along with whatever the most dominant persons have to say. Communities that do not experience open ideological conflict in the planning of change will reap hidden conflicts in implementation. Resistance, second-guessing, and subversion often uncover what has remained quietly under the surface. Thus what seems, at first glance, counterproductive becomes what is most productive —

the active encouragement of debate, differences of opinion, and discussion of the pros and cons of various contemplated actions. To maximize conflict at the beginning, in a thoughtful and informed way, is often to minimize dysfunctional conflict at the end.

It is important to realize, however, that productive conflict is *ideological* conflict — willing and open disagreement over ideas — not insults and character assassination. The road to school renewal is to invite and provide for constructive ways in which people can differ from one another. Those who are concerned about improving the quality of education must accept and steady themselves for a number of relatively unusual and uncomfortable developments; ideological conflict, when it appears, indicates progress. Other occurrences will also create tension, whether internal or external to the school. When tension is expected, accepted, and worked through, it can provide information and have positive results. When tension is unexpected, it can strike so suddenly and so hard that progress is destroyed.

School renewal is not a process of tripping merrily along a well-defined path strewn with rose petals. It is more like cutting a path of one's own through thick brambles. One can avoid excessive scratching and cuts by knowing where the thorns are.

Internal Pain of Autonomy

There is an intellectual headiness when members of a school community are given responsibility to govern themselves and determine the best educational practices. The euphoric state quickly diminishes when people realize that they can actually do what they really want to do. School people are conditioned to depend on external authorities, which have always circumscribed what schools can and cannot do. Autonomy is quite hard to believe in, and people are used to imagining what they could do "if only." When there is no "enemy" curtailing behavior, the responsibility for one's freedom can be frightening.

If a school wants a different curriculum, a different way of organizing time or documenting student performance, or a different classroom ratio, no external authority will tell them they cannot have it. Instead, the school as a community simply has to agree to make hard choices about current operations, current positions, and current use of time and monies. If there are "enemies" now that are keeping a school back, the "enemies" are themselves — their own collective will to change. In confronting the collective autonomy to act, there are profound questions about current educational practices that need to be openly debated.[1]

Homogeneous, Ability-Grouped Classes and Tracks

Most of the research indicates that placing students into ability groups does more educational harm than good for most (if not all) students. Lower-track students, once placed, hardly ever move into the higher tracks. They are taught less and challenged less, and they quickly learn to lower their expectations. They doubt their ability to succeed. Furthermore, students tend to be placed in lower-track classes more because of socioeconomic status and race than academic ability. There is often no prior statistical difference in achievement between students placed in the lower tracks and those just higher. Lower-performing students do worse when tracked and better when not tracked; higher-performing students do as well within mixed groups. This fact has applications to within-classroom grouping (breaking a single classroom into different ability groups) and across-classroom grouping. How does the school's current grouping of students work? Is the current operation fair? How can it be changed to minimize ability grouping but still provide for individual and group attention according to student needs? These are the questions for the school to ponder.

Subject-Based Curriculum

Curricula in many schools are structured by separate subjects, and learning in most schools is organized by separate disciplines, but most learning that students and adults do outside school is interdisciplinary. People deal with life issues and solve them from multiple perspectives and information sources.

Does the school's current curriculum reflect how people

really learn in the outside world? How can the curriculum reach across disciplines and still ensure that the important content, knowledge, and skills of separate disciplines are taught? Does the use of daily blocks of time and weekly schedules for teaching represent the best way for students to learn? These are questions for the school to consider.

Grade Levels, Unit Credits, and Grades

The use of grade levels was imported from Prussia in the early nineteenth century as a way of ranking and sorting students and standardizing American education during an influx of immigrants. Similarly, the unit credit was imposed on secondary schools to standardize college admission requirements. Grades come from a tradition of weighing and ranking students according to supposedly objective psychometric scales. All these conventions have become sacred cows. A school that is considering how best to develop an educational environment consistent with its principles of learning needs to probe and scrutinize its current practices. Is there really such an objective thing as a grade level or grade-level work? Could students be organized into other types of units? Do grades really reflect what students have learned and should be learning and what will be most helpful? Does any unit of credit reveal anything other than that a student has spent time in a classroom and received a passing grade? Could units or credits reflect actual performance, regardless of time spent in classes?

Textbooks and Classrooms

Outside school, most students and adults learn through "live" or archival materials — radio, television, newspapers, magazines, books, physical objects, computers, videos, and telephones. Very rarely does an adult go to an academic textbook to look something up or learn more about an issue, yet many schools spend most of their instructional money on textbooks, workbooks, and worksheets. This reliance on antiquated material keeps commercial publishers happy, gives the district and the state the appearance of providing uniform and consistent education for all students, and comforts teachers who have long relied on preordained structures. The typical learning environment is a four-walled classroom that a teacher and twenty to thirty students occupy for a set period of time. In many ways, learning in such a confined space is also an artificial departure from how people learn and interact in everyday life. Most offices, corporations, factories, homes, and communities arrange physical space to encourage a flow of people to various resources and information. No educational research has ever documented that the best way for students to learn is in a closed classroom with one teacher, yet that arrangement predominates in schools. Perhaps it exists more to control students than to help them. Do the school's current materials reflect the learning materials of present and future society? Does the current use of classroom and other physical space accord with how students actually learn? These are two questions for the school to consider.

Staffing

More than 80 percent of the typical school's budget is spent on personnel. Staff assignments have been shaped by bureaucratic notions of hierarchy. Therefore, there are secretaries, teacher aides, specialists, classroom teachers, principals, assistant principals, central office personnel, and superintendents. Role specialization was borrowed from the factory, where it was intended to monitor assembly-line work. It is not at all clear that such role specialization has ever been the best way to educate students. The number of students per teacher could drop dramatically if faculty in high schools taught for extended blocks of time with the same students, and if more specialized and administrative personnel at the school and district levels were reduced or took on part-time teaching roles. The typical use of one teacher for twenty to thirty students in an elementary or middle school also limits other potentially powerful ways to educate students. When a teacher resigns from a school, why automatically hire another? Perhaps that salary could be reallocated to several intern teachers working with a master teacher. Perhaps a team of teachers could work with the same number of students over several years, or several teachers could work part-time, with flexible hours. If an administrator resigns, why automatically hire a replacement, without thinking first of the *functions* of the position and seeing if its functions could be reassigned, to give more resources to the instructional program? Does the school's current staffing make educational sense? What important functions are needed to serve the educational program? How could staff provisions be reorganized to address those functions better? These are some questions for the school to think about.

Time

One of the more highly visible efforts at school reform has involved the rethinking of school time. Should a high school day be four, six, or seven periods long? In a middle school, should time be allocated flexibly so that teaching teams could decide on their own weekly or quarterly schedules? Should schools have community service days? Should school start earlier in the year and extend later? Should there be evening and weekend options for students? Should school be a year-round affair, with forty-five days on and fifteen days off so as to avoid a long summer vacation and its interruption of students' education? Another issue of school time has to do with the stability of being with the same group for several years. This issue is particularly prominent in schools with large numbers of students and highly mobile populations. For what *educational* reason should teachers and students have to develop whole new routines, expectations, and relationships every fall? Why can't students stay with one another and the same teacher or teachers for two, three, or more years? Does the current schedule for the school's day and year reflect how students learn best? Does the grouping of students and teachers over the years reflect how students learn best? All these issues involving time suggest that the school consider these questions.

Avoiding the Easy Route

When a school sets up a governing process and a governance structure, it is going to be controversial. Everyone thinks that his or her job and way of working is essential, and everyone basically thinks that the problems are with others. Hard questions, simply by being raised, challenge the status quo and elicit defensiveness, rationalizations, and sometimes outright anger. This is why conflict is both unavoidable and desirable: sensitivities can be expressed, and serious study and planning can proceed. Although my personal preferences should be clear by now, the answers to hard questions must come from the critical-study process of the school community, using its governance structure and covenant, not from outsiders — from the moral authority of the school, not from imposed authority.

People in a school must ask, "If we had no traditions or routines and could start with an empty building, what would our school look like, and how would it operate to fully prepare our students to become productive citizens of a democracy?" The dream creates excitement, but the details collide with reality. Initially, at least, most schools do not reach consensus on the schoolwide changes to be made. Some people argue for less ability-based grouping, some for more; others fight for flexible time, an integrated curriculum, and reality-based teaching materials. Still others defend the need for set periods of time, clearly separate subjects, and standard textbooks. Here the battle is joined, and the need for internal resolution is the first test of a school.

To meet the battle head-on, stay true to previous agreements, and gain momentum, the school needs to return to the core principles of learning. The pivotal dimension of resolution is the critical-study process. The debate should not be about opinions. It should seek to find out whether proposed changes would be of educational benefit. What must be read, heard, visited, and seen before final decisions are made? If, after the members have done their homework, the battle is still deadlocked, the school needs to continue study while moving ahead with some degree of implementation. Recall the guiding rules of governance: everyone *can* be involved in decision making, no one *has* to be involved, and, once a decision is made, everyone must support it.

Even partial schoolwide implementation gives enough concrete activities to be tested that, later on, people can reflect and decide whether the change has been positive and warrant more comprehensive implementation. If the battle is over less use of textbooks and more use of other teaching materials, then the school can decide either to implement the change fully, give each faculty member the chance to implement the change to some degree, commission a few faculty members to pilot the change, or not make the change at all. All but the last option keeps change moving. This range of options, even when there is great resistance, gives everyone the opportunity to pick a point on a continuum that everyone has agreed to. The reason to strive for schoolwide implementation, even when it is partial, is that this gives reluctant people a chance to try the change and gives more enthusiastic people the opportunity to forge ahead.

Schoolwide Resolution

Schoolwide change does not occur by default. Letting people do whatever they wish, or allowing small groups of faculty members to pilot programs without the endorsement of the entire school, is a mistake. To gain power *as* a school, the school as a whole must be working toward a common purpose. A schoolwide decision to let everyone "be eclectic" in reaching a school goal reflects an absence of moral and collective leadership. The most common and most mistaken response to conflict in a school is to avoid it, let people do what they wish, and develop a "school within a school." The latter response seems like the easiest way out of overt conflict, but it is no way out at all. Without the conscious, deliberate support of the entire school community, the "school within a school" causes further hardening, fragmentation, and divisiveness among faculty. The small group of enthusiastic teachers plows ahead, works hard and long, hears derisive comments from colleagues, and wears down after a time. The rest of the school does not care about what they do and does not want to learn from it, and the "school within a school" has no influence on the rest of the school. This is the sad legacy of such pilot programs.[2] A "school within a school" can work, however, if it has been commissioned through the governance process as consistent with the school's goals and priorities. Active approval and support from the rest of the school includes helping the program work, visiting and observing it, giving others opportunities to participate, and agreeing to study it as a prototype for later schoolwide implementation. This process ensures the program's influence. The pilot program becomes integral, a supported and studied activity of the entire school, rather than a capitulation to unresolved tension.

External Perils

There is a popular belief that competition among public schools — through tuition vouchers and student or parent choice plans — is the needed ingredient for improving education, but the opposite is true. Our public schools are and always have been competitive with one another. The competition exists both within and across school districts. Listen as school faculty, students, administrators, or parents talk about other schools. High schools and middle schools are constantly comparing themselves with their scholastic and athletic rivals. Elementary schools are highly sensitive to the program, work conditions, and community or district support that they and other schools receive. Sensitivity to standardized test scores published in newspapers verges on paranoia. Schools are ranked in school people's minds, as well as in real-estate sales pitches. To say that public schools suffer from lack of comparison and lack of pressure to outperform one another is virtual nonsense. Without taking a position on choice plans as such, let me just state that a significant issue in school renewal is the *lessening* of competition among schools, the breaking of schools' isolation, and the removal of dysfunctional types of interschool politics, so that schools can learn from one another without fear of comparison and reprisals (see also Glickman, Allen, and Lunsford, 1992).

In the existing climate of competition, schools that choose to move ahead with school renewal, forging a unique vision of teaching and learning, are more apt to be criticized and ostracized than praised and supported. Schools resent hearing about other schools where teachers, administrators, parents, and students are working together on unusual and progressive educational changes. Principals do not like to hear about other principals who share equally in decision making. Teachers do not like to find out that teachers in other schools have real power and do not use the same assessments, curricula, teaching materials, and teaching approaches of most schools.

The forging ahead of one school raises unsettling questions in other schools that are not forging ahead. Musings, often in public, range from "Why do they get to do it that way, and we do not?" to "Who do they think they are, creating their own program?" to "I would die or give my left arm to be at that school."

Interschool competition creates an interesting dilemma for school districts (see Chapter Eight). More relevant for now is the question of how a school that is struggling successfully with the core purpose of education should respond to other schools that are publicly critical and oppositional. The following suggestions are for schools involved in their own renewal.[3]

1. Listen carefully to the criticism, and decide whether it has any merit. For example, a school may receive great publicity for an effort that does not really deserve the publicity; it may be quite premature. If so, the school needs to acknowledge that it is still in the trial period. Other criticisms sometimes arise from schools where teachers, administrators, and parents believe that they are working just as hard but receiving little attention for their efforts. If so, then the recognized school often needs to acknowledge that it is only one of many schools doing such work, and that the recognition ought to be spread around.

2. Acknowledge publicly to other schools the good and the bad of the efforts and the struggles ahead. A school is simply setting itself up for further criticism if principals or teachers speak of their work as representing a model worthy of emulation by other schools. No school is without its warts and blemishes. It is more honest and helpful to other schools to let them see the whole picture of change and thus help them empathize with difficult realities.

3. Build professional craft knowledge across schools by exchanging visits. When people from other schools have an

opportunity to see a school at work in unstaged settings (classrooms, meetings) and have a chance to discuss the experience afterward, their understanding is more complete. More important, they see how schools can learn from one another.

In short, when schools are becoming more democratic, purposeful, and professional, the process must be demystified. Renewing schools must learn to accept criticism and difference. Virtually all schools have caring and hardworking people who wish to do well for students. The idea is not to put such people and schools on the defensive and thus stoke interschool rivalries, which may threaten one's own school. Instead, the solution is to demonstrate that schools are in the same boat and can be resources for one another as they try to determine what works best for their students.

The Principal: Captain of the Ship, or Democratic Wimp?

The principal of a renewing school, usually its most visible public figure, can become a lightning rod for controversy and disparaging remarks. It is ironic that when a principal initiates the most fulfilling way to serve the aims of education by being democratic in leadership, he or she is often regarded by others as extremely good, extremely bad, or entirely wacky. It is sometimes hard to understand how Americans have come to believe that public schools commissioned to prepare future citizens for a democracy should not be governed democratically. I know of principals to whom other principals have posed such questions as "You don't really *share* those decisions, do you? You do have a way, don't you, to make people think that your decisions are joint decisions?" and "Aren't you legally responsible for your school? How can you accept a decision that is counter to what you believe?" The more common statement is "You are the captain of the ship—the buck must stop with you." Years ago, I knew of an experienced principal who was just beginning to initiate democratic governance. He was embarrassed to tell other principals, for fear that they would laugh and make fun of him.

(These days, he regularly gives keynote speeches to conferences of state and national school administrators.) It is incredibly hard for many people to accept that a principal can or even should be democratic. How the principal handles such incredulity is crucial to the further establishment and acceptance of democratic practices among other school administrators. Successful principals handle the incredulous with statements such as these:

"I, as a principal, chose to engage in a democratic process; no one forced me."

"I, as a principal, am legally and ultimately responsible for decisions in our school." (This is not necessarily the case in some districts, of course, where policies make the school community the legal entity.)

"I, as a principal, am responsible to see that the best educational decisions possible get made, and I believe that this is best done by all of us, rather than by me alone."

"I, as a principal, am willing to occasionally lose on an issue that I strongly believe so that we all win as a school by becoming a powerful community."

"I, as a principal, acknowledge that this type of democratic governance is not every principal's or school's cup of tea at the moment, but it is what I believe all of us should be striving for."

Similar responses could be made by teachers, aides, specialists, parents, and students.

Obviously, a single person should not be receiving all the recognition and all the criticism of a renewing school. For many reasons, it is better that a renewing school be represented during forums, presentations, and visits by several people besides the principal who represent the schoolwide effort.

Perils in the Larger Community

Virtually every community person has an opinion about public schools; after all, almost everyone went to one. The same townspeople who unblinkingly accept changes in transportation, communication, farming, and commerce have difficulty imagining that a school can be anything other than what it has always been — an amalgam of classrooms, teachers, textbooks, grade levels, test scores, and unit credits. When a school starts to alter these conventions, it can expect some negative reactions from the town.

If students are engaged in real and active work and are involved in community learning, with flexible time and new forms of assessment, some people will not understand these changes and will dislike what is being done, no matter how well the school has involved parents, caretakers, and the community in the decisions for change. Here is where the matter becomes more interesting. The general public has been led to believe that schools are going down the drain and doing terrible things to students. In poll after poll, the surveyed public agrees that dramatic changes have to be made. Commission reports at the federal and state levels urge the need for "shock waves." "Restructuring" and "breaking the mold" are proclaimed as the saviors of America's economy, labor force, and international markets, yet when individual schools take these ideas seriously and develop bold new ways of educating students, the general public, through a group of parents or concerned citizens, often goes to the district or the school board to "stop all this nonsense." The message, borne out by many polls, is that people feel that all schools should be innovative — except for their local schools.

Thus renewing schools are caught in a bind. They are urged to "go for it," but the local community does not want change. It is easy to portray this scenario as one of good, enlightened school community members versus bad, misguided townspeople, but the situation is more complex. A bold school should expect controversy from parents, caretakers, and community persons. If not, the change is probably not very bold. A conventional, ordinary school that offers endless pap is often untouched by controversy, and parents who do not like it learn to be quiet or move. Community people who do not think much *of* a mundane school do not tend to do much *about* it. Unless the town budget is tight or the school is rocked by violence or drugs, the educational program goes unnoticed. To the stronghearted, change-oriented school comes the peril.

Why Peril?

A school, with its charter, has involved parents and community members in decision making. It has developed a covenant of learning principles and, through critical study, it has sampled additional parental and community responses to proposed actions. Those parents and community members who get involved typically become strong advocates of change and help school personnel inform the larger community. People involved in the process tend to reason more than those who are not involved about benefits for all children. Those who have not been part of the process tend to view the changes in terms of the immediate effects on their own children, their tax rates, or the disruption of their lives. People outside the process often do not have the same level of understanding and are thus more susceptible to rumors of disastrous consequences. The situation is not helped if a few individuals inside the school use their own dislike of decisions to rally outsiders to their cause. Public controversy about schoolwide change, to be handled productively, must be considered from several perspectives.

First, does the degree of controversy indicate general failure of the school to communicate and to consider outside feedback before making schoolwide decisions? If so, there may be a need for a temporary stay, further study, and a deadline for reconsidered action.

Second, does the source of the controversy come down to relatively few, vocal dissidents who have very personal concerns? If so, how can the school listen to those individual concerns and address them so as to continue with the major changes? For example, are there parents who would thwart an entire program because they do not want their own children to participate? Could options be offered to those parents without compromising the entire program? Could those parents move their children to another school? Could parents be asked to give the program a chance for a certain period, after which the program would be reviewed and other options, as necessary, would be explored? If the issue is with people in the community other than parents, could some of the same solutions apply? For example, if some townspeople do not like a new program (students working in downtown internships or involved in classroom studies of community issues, such as homeless people, the environment, or local zoning ordinances), could the program be phased in so that the town can see how it will operate?

Third, regardless of the extent and degree of discontent, criticism should always be listened to and considered. It may suggest a new option that has never been thought about before. It may suggest a more inclusive process for the future. It may bring new and different perceptions to future plans and decisions.

Most important, if everyone learns from public controversy, it brings power and wisdom to the next set of decisions. If a school tends to ignore or downplay criticism, a controversy can recur until the school's energy is sapped.

Crisis Points

Historians always have the luxury of looking back on revolutions, to determine the key events and the decisions that gave momentum and power to the cause. After twenty-five years of working with schools on sustained school renewal, I have the luxury of pointing out some key moments that have sustained democratic education. This list of key moments is not inclusive; I am sure that readers could add many moments of their own. Furthermore, this list does not minimize the anguish that people have experienced in dealing with crisis points. At best, it says that a school community in turmoil is in good company. Other schools have moved through similar crises, to emerge stronger than before. It is in how a school deals with crisis that all is won or all is lost. Crises have to occur in order for a school to clarify its beliefs and its commiment to education as a moral enterprise.

Crisis 1: Losing to Gain

A critical moment in a school community comes when people see that the governance process will be abided by: the principal loses on a decision that he or she has strongly opposed. It is only at such a time that others understand, intellectually and emotionally, that the process is for real. The clarifying moment occurs when the principal has made his or her opposition known, has fought hard to convince and influence others, and then says, "I disagree. I do not think we should do that this way, but as a member of this group, with the same vote as anyone else, I will abide by the decision and work as hard as I can to make it successful."

Crisis 2: Picking Up the Pieces

A governance meeting is in shambles. People are rude to one another. They ignore one another's point of view. No priorities or actions are set; complaining, whining, and resentment are evident. The meeting goes nowhere, and everyone leaves unhappy. The critical juncture comes at the follow-up meeting, when someone in the group (often a teacher) has the courage to openly express the general frustration: "It is not worth any of our time if our meetings are going to be like the last one. I want to apologize for my own actions. I realize that we may never work together in total harmony, but can we figure out how to be more productive than in the past?" Regardless of who brings the sore points up, frustration is ventilated, and a working plan for better group dynamics emerges.

Crisis 3: Being Attacked

The crisis of dealing with private or public attacks by persons from other schools, from one's own group, from parents or community members, or from school district officials hinges on the school's response. The instinctive response is to circle the wagons, to claim one's school as the sole proprietor of righteousness and wisdom, and to attack the attackers as stupid and immoral. This instinct must be consciously checked. Instead, the school needs to exhibit an attitude of listening, understanding, and discussion with the attackers. Successful schools continue to work through this kind of crisis without aggressive retorts, even when attacks enter the newspapers and other media. The school's response is measured, calm, and dignified. School people acknowledge the right of others to their opinions. They correct information that is erroneous. They do not put themselves on a pedestal. They are open to suggestions, but they stick to their core educational beliefs and do not compromise what they see as educationally right. They take the time to explain and be available to those who desire more information, and they let it be known that what they are trying to accomplish will take time. There will be glitches along the way, and they will carefully study and modify their original plans, as necessary.

Crisis 4: "It Would Be Great, But . . . "

Another crisis involves the "hesitancy gap" that many schools experience in moving from the theory to the reality of implementation. Usually by the third year after implementing the covenant, the charter, and the critical-study process, schools are ready to deal with hard questions and to dream about the ideal school. Predictably, when consensus on the ideal is reached, the plan starts to break down in the details of personal change. ("What? You mean I will have to move to another room?") Members then slow down their initial enthusiasm for bold change and find it easier to say, "Let us think more about this. Maybe we really should not do it." Most schools, in the first few years of renewal, are ready for incremental change—improving on the existing structure. Schools with several years' experience implementing incremental change are ready for major changes. The critical junction comes in acknowledging people's individual fears as a natural stage of entering new territory and finding out ways of easing the change for each person. At the end, people hold one another's hands and take the plunge.

Time, Surges, and the Rainbow

School renewal is not a linear progression, a smooth ascent to betterment. Rather, school renewal is more like a series of surges and lulls over an extended period. At any fixed point, improvement may not be apparent, but in the long haul there is no question about progress. By *surges,* I mean periods of excitement, frenzied activity, and great expenditure of human energy. By *lulls,* I mean intermittent periods of quiet, consolidation of work, and conservation of energy. In short, school renewal is human activity, with all the characteristics of human moods and rhythms, ranging from elation to despair, from working hard to resting, from seriousness to playfulness, from happiness to sorrow, and from crisis to tranquillity. At the end of the episodic showers, thunder, and lightning, the rainbow becomes apparent. In the orchestration of human energy within a solid structure of democratic learning principles, powerful education is achieved.

Chapter Eight

Supporting School Renewal: The District's Role

A major shift in the organization, design, and responsibilities of school districts will be needed to institutionalize school renewal as an incessant activity for all schools in a state and a nation. There can be no long-term rethinking of schools if there is not a long-term rethinking of the central policies and support structures provided to schools. The central issues between schools and districts are those of control and responsibility. Who is in charge of what? Who initiates what? Who is responsible for what? Who supports whom? In answering these questions, a delicate balance is needed for districts to be able to support schools that have developed a democratic community, ready to move ahead and provide control and structure to those schools not yet ready for collective autonomy. Districts should not separate the two groups of schools into rival camps.

The need for clear policies that strike a balance between autonomy and control at the district level is a great challenge, one that many school boards, teachers' unions and associations, and superintendents and district personnel have just begun to understand. From the school board's and the district's perspective, it is fairly easy to determine what is wrong and should be corrected in local schools. It is more difficult to see what is wrong with the district and the board. Self-analysis must precede the casting of the first stone.

This analysis must be carefully thought through, or else

the entire school-based reform movement will be added to the long list of innovations that have come and gone. The lack of such thought and sensitivity to the complexities, differences, and histories of school reform has been seen, time and again, in the treatment of local schools by many superintendents, school boards, districts, and unions. This time, the new solution is to mandate that all schools become site-based, decentralized, and collaborative by a particular date. Furthermore, these new regulations, with the same old top-down strategy, go on to define the same governance process, composition, and role for all schools. One shoe, even though the shoe is new, is still supposed to fit everyone.

This new trend has been sweeping the country, but if we study carefully how successful democratic communities are formed, we will realize that to mandate decentralization is absurd. This is another case of a simplistic approach to the fragile human and moral enterprise of schools. Pause for a moment, and think about mandating that a school be site-based and decentralized, without seeing first whether the local school members are ready or willing to take greater control over themselves. Imagine how implausible it is to require that all schools be collaborative and then to define their governance for them, without involving the schools themselves in determining their own forms, processes, and principles of governance. Most site-based policies in states and districts are simply seen as requirements pushed down the throats of local school people, who are told by decree that they will be democratic, like it or not.

Democracies and moral enterprises do not work that way. Enduring democracies are not created by uniform mandates. Such policies are simply old wine in new bottles, which will be tasted but not swallowed — simply regurgitated, as in the past. Democracies that stand the test of time and remain consistent to their core functions are created from within.[1] Covenants are developed, charters are instituted, and a built-in process of critical study and reflection is implemented by the local people themselves. Democracies that succeed are of the people, by the people, and for the people.

What Does a School Board or District Want?

I would suggest that the only legitimate role of school boards and districts is to ensure that students are being educated to become productive citizens of the larger society. The school board's role is one of setting broad policies and providing resources that support schools' ability to accomplish that goal. The district's role is to coordinate and implement active assistance to schools. Let me be clear, at the risk of sounding incredibly naïve: the role of the school board is not to be involved in the internal educational operations of the school, and the role of the districts is not to determine for students, teachers, principals, and parents the educational programs of a school. The job of both board and district is to define the district's core beliefs about teaching and learning; define the goals and objectives (outcomes) of an educated student; provide the money, technical services, and human consultation to allow schools to figure out how to get the job done; and determine whether progress is being achieved. They should intervene into the programs and operations of schools when they are asked by the school to do so, when the school is not prepared to make decisions for itself, or when a mutually agreed-upon degree of progress is not forthcoming.

For the first time in American education, there is a serious national movement that questions the need for districts and school boards. Other countries, such as New Zealand and England, have either eliminated school boards and districts completely or allowed individual schools simply to leave their districts. Similar experiments are occurring in North America. It will be a sad day in American democracy if school boards and public officials elected to look after the common good in education are deemed irrelevant. It will be a loss of potential assistance if school districts that could serve a vital role, by assisting schools in their internal work, are discarded. What will be needed is a move away from the nineteenth-century mentality of standardizing and controlling schools to a twenty-first century mentality of response and assistance within principled parameters.

Why Get in the Way?

What would be lost, and what would be gained, if a district were to tell its schools that they could have total latitude with programs and funds if they operated within the following givens?

- Constitutional law
- Equity for all students
- Multicultural sensitivity
- Attention to research
- Progress toward district goals
- Public disclosure of student results
- Foundation of a school covenant, charter, and critical-study process

What these givens suggest is that a school board and a district would want to give their schools autonomy if the schools had a foundation for making decisions, if those decisions were made within responsible and legal parameters, and if student results were consistent with district priorities and were made public. Let us elaborate on the givens. *Constitutional law* implies that whatever the school chooses to do is not in violation of state or federal laws. *Equity for all students* means that educational decisions take account of the education of all students; they do not favor one group of students at the expense of others, and they narrow existing gaps in achievement among groups of students. *Multicultural sensitivity* implies that school decisions must respond to racial, ethnic, cultural, and gender differences and incorporate related issues into teaching and learning. *Attention to research* is defined as a basis of empirical and case-study evidence to support particular decisions and as evidence of a process for monitoring the results of the decision. *Progress toward district goals* implies that a school's decisions will somehow address those educational priorities that exist across all schools within the district and that have the school board's approval. *Public disclosure of student results* refers to the school's responsibility to make known, through public meetings, printed reports, and district or school board briefings, attainment or progress toward identified objectives and priorities. *Foundation of a school covenant, charter, and critical-study process* refers to the school plan's having been derived from democratic governance, from the school's principles of teaching and learning, and from a systematic method of information infusion, study, and action research. A district may wish to enlarge on, expand, clarify, or reduce these givens, or it may wish to start from scratch and come up with its own givens. The reader may be following merrily along, saying, "No big deal — this sounds fine as district policy. We could do this." Here comes the jolt to school districts and boards: if a board or a district is correctly focused on parameters, processes, and results, and if individual schools accept the givens and develop their plans, then the details and programs are up to the schools.

This means that a school could use different teaching materials, organize students differently, use school time differently, spend money differently, and staff differently from other schools in the same district. Assessment of student learning could vary, grades and report cards could be unique and released at different times, and the curriculum could vary from school to school. One high school could have eight periods, with an open campus; another could have four periods, with a closed campus. One school could teach by traditional disciplines; another, by spiral themes. One school could develop and use its planning time, staff development money, and teacher evaluation procedures differently from others. One school could adopt a textbook series; others would not have to. One school could reduce its administrative staff and give faculty extended contracts; another could reduce the teaching faculty and increase counseling and social services. Schools would be free to enter into their own agreements with granting agencies, community services, and businesses. Groups of schools could band together to coordinate services among themselves. The district's role in such unshackling would be to provide information and potential services, uncover common needs, and coordinate and link resources to those schools that have emerged from their own assessments and plans.

If this sounds like anarchy, remember that we are dealing only with schools that are ready for such work, have prepared their own communities for doing such work, and desire to become more democratic and participative. These are schools with a purpose. We are not talking about schools that are neither inclined toward or ready for such work. Obviously, they will need more central structure, control, and preparation before they undertake the transition to democratic, site-based school renewal.

Accountability: The School Board and the District

Before we proceed to specific policy formation, the concepts of fairness and sameness need to be untangled. That schools might be allowed, within set parameters, to have unique curricula, teaching materials, staffing, schedules, and reports disturbs some highly caring people. They have a keen sense of social justice for all students in their districts, and they equate justice with equal treatment. Their thinking is expressed in this way: "To show that we do not discriminate, or teach any student from any part of town less than any student from other parts of town, we, as a school board and district, need to ensure that all students receive the same programs, the same curriculum, the same textbooks, and the same allocations of time. Therefore, fifth-grade work is fifth-grade work, no matter what school a student attends, and a high school course of study is the same course of study, no matter what high school a student attends." The idea, well-intentioned and understandable, is that fairness to students means treating all students alike.

Without taking this point to extremes, I would like to suggest the opposite: to be fair to students, we need to have different treatments, because our concern should be with the *fairness of results,* not the *sameness of treatment.* Look at virtually any school district with more than three or four schools, where the same programs are given to all students, and you will find many students falling farther and farther behind in educational results the longer they receive the same treatment. A district is in the indefensible position of arguing for and controlling uniformity of programs across schools while sizable portions of students lose their motivation to learn.

It is fairer and more just for a district to focus on the uniformity of a broad outcome — a productive, democratic citizenry — than to demand compliance with identical treatment by monitoring and testing for a list of competencies and skills, to see that everyone in the district is covering the same objectives in the same sequence, divorced from democratic life.

The legitimate role of a district, superintendent, and school board is to address the concern for fairness by allowing willing schools to have the latitude to produce equitable results, keeping structure and consistent programs in place for schools currently unable or unwilling to initiate, and adjusting resources to account for equity of results.

It is in the adjustment of resources that, again, unequal treatment becomes most fair. Those schools in a district that have the highest percentages of students in poverty should receive the largest allocation of funds. To allocate the same funds equally on the basis of enrollment perpetuates the existing inequities in education. A district should strive to make its high-poverty schools the most attractive ones, by offering additional resources, nicer facilities, supplements and incentives for faculty and staff, and more staff development opportunities. In this way, a district does not neglect its higher-income schools but acknowledges that the challenges a high-income school community faces are simply not the same as those in poor schools. This may be politically unpopular, since vocal parents, community members, and school board members disproportionately come from the wealthier part of town or see themselves as representing the higher-income and highly educated segment of the community and want equal or even more funds to flow to their schools and their children. But a district and board concerned about justice and fairness needs to think of unequal distribution of funds as a way to correct glaring inequities of educational progress.

In the same manner, a district should set aside some funds as *venture capital,* to be used as seed money to help schools wishing to take steps toward operating as autonomous, responsible communities. The venture capital could be a small percentage of the district budget or a semi-independent budget of outside funds raised from donations, grants, and corporate or business sponsorships. The venture capital should be enough so that a school could use it to pay for some extra planning days, retreats, off-site facilities, or staff development opportunities, to help provide additional planning for school change.

It is difficult to set an exact dollar amount, but venture capital of as little as $500 to $1,000 for a school can be helpful in the beginning year. A more adequate fund for a large school would be up to $10,000. Venture capital should be targeted only to schools that have indicated a willingness to accept the conditions for autonomy (the givens), and the capital is provided on an as-needed basis, with schools in poverty areas having greatest priority. Ideally, venture capital should be provided for the first few years of implementation, with the school eventually operating on its normally allotted funds and thus freeing venture capital for other schools.

There are no hard and fast rules about the amount or duration of venture capital. Districts that simply do not have money for such an enterprise and have no way to raise it can still proceed with an invitation for their schools to regulate themselves under certain parameters, with the district committing certain services to the schools. Venture capital is most important as a symbol of support, as inadequate in dollars as that might be. The district is acknowledging the extra time and work involved in a school's becoming a community and providing a token of support, to be used by the school for its planning.

Just as important, venture capital should never be used to exclude or limit the number of schools that want to participate in school renewal. It is better to provide no money, thus allowing any and all schools that want to participate, than to provide money for only a few schools and thus eliminate others from participating. A district needs to make invitational policies of decentralized school renewal accessible and available to all schools and must avoid the creation of pilot programs that divide the district into "elite" schools and have-nots. This is tricky when money is attached to participation. The district would need to decide that every school that initiates a proposal could receive some additional funds, that no school would receive funds, or that only schools meeting more specific criteria (high percentages of poor students) would receive funds.

Identifying the Readiness of Schools

Table 8.1 may clarify schools' readiness to become successful, democratic communities. Level 1 represents a school where there

Table 8.1. Levels of Readiness.

	1	2	3	4	5
Knowledge	Don't know	Don't know	Know	Know	Know
Commitment	Don't care	Care	Care	Care	Care
History of collaboration	None	None	None	Some	Total
Readiness	Not ready	Not ready	Not ready	Ready for entry	Full implementation
Needed structure	District structure	District structure	District structure	Self-governance	Self-governance

is little knowledge about how to improve schoolwide education and there is little commitment to or caring about finding out what can be done. Level 2 represents a school where there is little knowledge about school renewal because the school has been highly isolated and routinized in the past, but there is interest among many people to find out what can be done. At level 3, school members are knowledgeable about schoolwide change, and there is a large group committed to change; schoolwide collaboration has just begun, and the school needs time to get its charter, covenant, and critical-study process in order. At level 4, the school possesses knowledge and commitment, has developed a democratic process for decision making, has identified principles of learning, has set learning targets, and is ready for implementation. At level 5, the school already is self-governing, with a record of accomplishment, and is now pursuing bolder changes. These classifications are artificial in that schools can slip and slide, backtrack, and leap forward. For the sake of clarifying school district policy, however, let us suppose that schools really are at these different levels of preparation, and that level 5 — full implementation — is what the district wants every school to achieve eventually. How does a district help every school move ahead, regardless of level of readiness? How can this be done if democracy must grow from the inside out, if the same treatment for all schools is inherently unfair, and if mandates are failure-prone?

A District Plan for Encouraging School Initiative

A district plan should acknowledge different levels of school readiness, send an invitation for schools to test their readiness for autonomy, provide special linking services to willing and ready schools, continue existing district regulation for schools that are not yet ready, keep access open so that all schools can learn from others, and increase the autonomy of each school until all schools are special places with uniquely crafted programs focused on democracy and learning.

Acknowledging Different Levels

Districts need to make clear to schools that they are not expected to do what they are not ready to do. History, traditions, norms, and routines vary from school to school, and the soundest way of bringing about school renewal is to ask schools to figure out for themselves whether they are willing and ready to proceed with self-governance around schoolwide educational changes. If they are not, it is no flaw in their character; it is simply an acknowledgment that they will need centralized district structures to guide their current work and will need further orientation for all roles in becoming more autonomous.

Sending an Invitation

There is no better way to find out what schools are ready to do than to ask them, by sending an invitation. It should make the following matters understandable:

- The criteria for self-governance (what has to be in place in the school)
- The district givens (the parameters of the school's work)
- The areas that the district will decentralize to the school (funding, evaluation, curriculum, scheduling)
- Particular resources and assistance that the district will commit to the school
- Evaluation (how the school will hold itself accountable for student results)
- The necessary assurances that the school has the commitment of the principal and of a high proportion of faculty and staff, as well as the involvement of parents and students

The full commitment of the principal is a must, and high faculty and staff commitment is also essential. Requiring a secret ballot among faculty and staff is an important way to block any potential undue influence or pressure.[2] In no case should a school receive district approval for schoolwide autonomy when the majority of faculty or staff are against it, or when the principal opposes it.

Prior measures of student performance should not be used as criteria for acceptance of a school into self-governance. Some districts and states have unwittingly ushered in self-renewal programs while selecting only schools with high student performance. Apart from the problems with performance indicators themselves, the test of the school's mettle should be whether the school is willing to engage in the struggle to figure out better ways of educating students. It can be argued, reasonably, that schools with lower student performance indicators need greater access to decentralized efforts than do schools that are doing relatively well in the public's and district's eyes.

Providing Linking Services

Venture capital can help schools with some of their own planning, and the district should provide coordinators for school renewal. Teams of approximately four to nine people from each school (the principal, a majority of faculty, parents and other community members, possibly students, and a district contact person) should be brought together periodically (at least once every ten weeks) to review processes with one another, meet with schools or consultants outside their districts to discuss similar changes, and spend time in internal discussions about and further planning for their own schools. The district should also provide a central office person as the school's contact person, to be called for assistance with needs assessment, information gathering, and participation in school meetings. Furthermore, the district should provide ways of formally linking the schools via newsletters, electronic mail, visits, and identification of school people with expertise who can consult with one another for workshops, on-site visits, curriculum work, and staff development.

Continuing Existing Regulations

A district should not throw the baby out with the bath water. Over time, the district has established policies and regulations that ensure at least minimal levels of competent instruction. Teacher evaluation programs, curriculum work, reporting procedures, staff development programs, hiring practices, and other district standards for school performance should not be discarded. Instead, they should serve as a template for all schools until all schools have developed willingness and a process and plan for moving beyond the template. Therefore, all the normal district standards and regulations remain in force for schools that are not yet ready to accept the invitation. This is not a punitive matter. Rather, it is a developmental matter of respecting the temporary need of some schools for protective external structures.

Keeping Access Open

To avoid the exclusionary and elitist fragmentation that occurs among schools in districts where pilot programs give some schools special status and recognition, the school district's policies should show that the opportunity to be self-governing is open to every school. All schools have the same opportunity to apply and be approved, and there are no limits on the number of schools that

can participate. A nonparticipating school can even opt in periodically. The door is never shut.

With such a plan, the district has the responsibility of
keeping all its schools informed of the others' work. Some ways
of keeping information flowing are to invite members from nonparticipating schools to attend district meetings of participating schools; encourage visits between participating and nonparticipating schools; disseminate newsletters, progress reports, and
other materials from participating schools to nonparticipating
schools; and publicly acknowledge good instructional work going on in nonparticipating schools. The last point is worth not-
ing: a district should not set up the instructional program of
the participating schools as the model that receives all the recognition; other schools may come to view those schools and the
district program with resentment, and nonparticipating schools
may come to believe that the district regards them as inferior.
One way to avoid or minimize this type of resentment is to show-
case exciting and valuable practices in all the schools, regardless of whether they are participating in self-renewal. There are
indeed exceptional programs that involve students in meaningful
and highly challenging work in some nonparticipating schools,
which may very well be equal or superior to those in self-renewal
schools. Therefore, to acknowledge and share such practices is
important.

Increasing Autonomy

As a district learns of successes and failures among self-renewing
schools, it should use this information to assess and modify current regulations in all the schools. For example, if one school
has found a novel and particularly effective way to deliver the
curriculum, that information should be used when the current
standard curriculum for the district comes up for review.

All in all, the district must make it clear that its policies
are meant to unleash the creativity and particular talents of each
school community. The district is concerned with students' becoming productive citizens in a democratic society. The result
of that process is the driving and ultimate concern. Some dis-

tricts are more conservative and will have many battles over turf. Both the schools and the district need to learn what to give up in order to gain for students. The bargain is that autonomy is granted within parameters, but the parameters are expanded as schools show their power to be successful. The goal is to have all schools exercising their own professional and moral judgments as school communities. No educational idea that has been carefully studied, that fits the givens, and that has the support of the local school community should be suppressed; it should be encouraged, supported, and assisted by the district.

Do the District and the Board Eventually Fade Away?

Paradoxically, as schools take on greater responsibility for themselves, the role of the school board and, more pointedly, the work of the central office increases. The district must reorganize itself, give more resources back to schools, and provide the coordination among schools that does not occur by chance. There will be fewer bureaucratic functions of the central office, in terms of chain of command and decisions made for schools, and there may be fewer personnel. The personnel who do remain will have a threefold job: keeping local school work focused on education, coordinating information across schools, and helping schools do the work that they cannot do by themselves. It is easier to sit in a central office and make decisions about what schools should do than to sit with schools and figure out how to help coordinate and implement their work.

Issues in Building District Policies

In working with various school districts throughout the United States, Canada, and Western Europe, I have found that several issues are important to resolve in the development of district plans for school renewal. The solutions provide a sense of overall purpose for individual schools in relation to the entire district, allowing all people to understand their responsibilities and to know when it is appropriate for the district to intervene in an individual school's affairs. These issues should be tackled, in the preliminary analysis, by the key representatives of the district: the superintendent, school board members, central office personnel, principals, teachers and, as appropriate, parent, community, civic, business, and student groups.

Issue 1: Who Is the District?

What does the district stand for? How are district decisions made that directly affect teaching and learning? How are district decisions studied to determine their effects on student learning? These questions deal with the substance of the district's covenant, charter, and critical-study process. The most important question concerns who the district is, since it influences all the rest. What does it mean to say, "This is a district decision"? Is it a decision made by the superintendent, alone or with the school board? with an administrative cabinet of assistant superintendents or directors? with a leadership council composed of central office and building principals? Or is it a decision using a defined process and body that fully represents all who are to be affected by the decision?

Issue 2: What Do Schools Clearly Control?

What areas of decision making simply belong to individual schools? They do not need to check with the district, and they do not need to ask permission. They simply make the decisions for themselves and keep the district informed about what has been done (Chapter Three discusses the various areas of decision making for a school). All parties must understand the kinds of decisions that clearly belong to individual schools (parent programs, scheduling, curriculum, report cards, budgeting and staffing, hiring of personnel, staff development, and so on).

Issue 3: What Does the School District Clearly Control?

This is the flip side of issue 2. What are the areas that individual schools cannot make decisions about (such as transportation, student transfer rules, school calendar, maintenance and custodial care, food services, allocation of financial resources to schools)?

Issue 4: What Are the Gray Areas?

These are the areas that are known to be unclear, which the district retains control over until a school actively pursues a waiver. For example, does the district currently make decisions in curriculum, testing, staff development, teacher evaluation, personnel hiring, graduation requirements, and categorical budget allocations? Do these decisions usually remain with the district unless a school submits a plan? How would the district initiate an invitation to a school to submit a plan to receive a waiver? With what parameters (givens) and in what ways would the district need to monitor whether the school carries through with its plan?

Issue 5: What Is the District's Commitment to Self-Renewing Schools?

How should the district be organized? What people and services (technical and logistical) will the district provide? Site-based decentralization in a school district is not simply a matter of saying, "You want greater control? Take it." Rather, it involves reciprocal responses by the district, to provide targeted assistance to help schools be successful.

Issue 6: What Responsibility Does the District Have to Schools That Are Not Ready?

What requirements must be kept in place (or developed) for schools that are not initiators? The district needs to be able to define the standards and structures for schools that do not now have a broad-based, democratic will toward self governance. Therefore, what basic programs (for curriculum, teaching materials, staff development, teacher evaluation, testing and reporting procedures) are required for schools that need structure, guidance, and mentoring?

Teachers' Unions and Associations

The decentralization of regulations (now held by districts, school boards, and state departments) to local schools is premised on the idea that the will of the local school community to be thoughtful, responsible, and purposeful should be paramount. If a school accepts the givens and, through its democratic process, finds better ways to organize and operate, external agencies should not stand in its way. Teachers' unions and associations have responsibilities similar to those of districts: not to obstruct but, instead, to help initiating schools. Teachers' organizations should have their own policies, making it clear that if the majority of people in a school (including, of course, the teachers) want to try out activities that are not in accord with negotiated contracts or union regulations, then the latter will be set aside.

In speaking about policy changes needed at the district level, I am also referring to changes in negotiated contracts. I am fully aware that regulations from teachers' own associations (about such issues as how often faculty can meet, for what length of time, and under what conditions) can become as restrictive of local school initiatives as district and school board policies. The recent emergence of negotiated "enabling contracts" is a healthy departure. These contracts, between unions and districts, allow individual schools the freedom not to follow previous agreements if certain givens are met.

Biting the Bullet with Decentralized Policies

District policies that focus on the primary purpose of public schools—to educate students for productive citizenship in a democracy—must focus on student learning and facilitate the democratic efforts of schools to move forward. Policy, at best, aids a local school community's own efforts to do moral work on behalf of students. At worst, policy obstructs and forces local school members to comply with work that they regard as immoral. In externally controlled and regulated schools, principals and teachers often say, "We know that what we are doing is not in the best interest of our students. It is not how students learn best, but it is what our district requires." What a terrible way to live a professional life! The moral dimension of living one's life in obligation to principles should be the core of the work of local schools. Educators, students, parents, and other concerned citizens should be deciding what is right, not how to comply with what is wrong.

When a district consciously promotes the moral work of schools by decentralizing, upon request, areas of decision making that previously were centralized, the transition can create confusion and frustration. When a school chooses to become democratic and take greater control, it also chooses to accept greater responsibility for its actions, and the district should not intervene when a school makes a controversial decision. This is one of the toughest lessons for schools and districts to learn when moving from dependence to independence. The following story is about a school in a district that had developed clear policies allowing schools to know what they controlled and how to gain greater control by responding to district invitations:

> The school asked for and received site-based autonomy over certain areas, including staff hiring, teaching materials, internal scheduling arrangements, and all matters of curriculum. The school members, after having established their covenant, charter, and critical-study process, determined a need for students to become more active constructors of knowledge. They found that the current curriculum did not involve all the modalities of learning necessary to the active construction of knowledge. The school put together a curriculum task force of teachers, staff, administrators, parents, and students to investigate recent advances in curriculum, and the task force visited other schools. Finally, the group recommended to the governing body a five-year plan for revitalizing the existing curriculum. One specific recommendation, which was approved, was to integrate physical education, art, and music with English, mathematics, and science through "webbed" student projects.

The first project in the first year was to have students develop an outdoor education facility in a corner of the schoolyard. Teachers from the various disciplines coordinated students' assignments. After six months of well-executed work, the students had planned, designed, budgeted, tested, and constructed a breathtaking outdoor space, which included an obstacle course, rope- and rock-climbing apparatus, a garden, and a greenhouse. Students wrote how-to manuals, produced a video, sent out their own news releases, held radio and television interviews, and volunteered to work with the town to convert other outdoor spaces for the town's use. They joined with adult civic groups and began to plan similar public spaces for abandoned lots and neglected parks.

Everything seemed fine. The students were involved, making applications of their learning and using the disciplines of math, science, English, art, and music. Then a homeowner called a school board member, demanding that the rope-and-rock-climbing structure be removed. In fact, she preferred to see the whole project dismantled; the apparatus had been built in her direct line of sight. She petitioned her neighbors about the "ugly" structure, the "horrendous" colors, the noise, and the obstruction of her view.

A school board member listened and directed the homeowner to speak to the principal. She did so and, after hearing the principal's explanation, was still unsatisfied and rallied her allies. They called other board members and insisted that the apparatus come down. The superintendent heard of the discontent from all sides: from board members, from the principal, and from the irate homeowners. At the next board meeting, the homeowners brought their formal complaint to the board, demanding action in open session.

Preventive measures might have been taken before this controversy escalated, but the scenario is most instructive. It shows the transition between the old impulse to keep schools as they are, dependent on the old power structure of centralized authority, and the new policy of responsible, school-based renewal. The old impulse says that whenever a school issue becomes publicly controversial, the superintendent or school board needs to take the matter over, consult with the parties, and decide the issue for them. The new, reasoned approach is to keep responsibility for the decision where policy stuck it — with the decision makers. Clearly, the district had delegated the areas of curriculum and use of physical space to the individual school; therefore, the decision was properly the school's to make, and any repercussions of the decision also belonged to the school. It was not up to the superintendent or the school board to resolve this issue. To do so would clearly have violated the school renewal policy and undermined belief in any future school renewal work, not only for this school but also for others. In this case, the superintendent and the board followed proper procedure:

> The superintendent reminded the board of the policy, and the board chair told the irate homeowners, "This is not our matter to decide. You need to go back to the school, ask for an appointment with the principal and the governing board of the school, restate and explain your grievance, and try to find a mutual resolution. If no resolution is forthcoming, and you and the school wish to have an outsider arbitrater, then such a person will be furnished. I appreciate your concern and look forward to hearing the results of your discussion."

The issue was resolved at the school level. The school's governing board learned a lesson about the need to gather more feedback before making changes that might affect people outside of the school. The credibility of school-based renewal remained, and the school and the district have since made strides in educational renewal.

Not all scenarios will unfold so simply and be resolved so clearly. The greatest dilemma for school districts and boards is the question of whether they really want to give schools responsibility and control through clear policies or whether they are ambivalent and so want to leave policies general and ambiguous. The latter route allows for much rhetoric but little substance in school renewal.

If districts do not take the time to develop clear policies, schools are left in a nowhere land, no different from before, buffeted by the winds of individual influence and personal favors, and knowing that their feet can be cut out from under them at any moment of public controversy, or that "the boss" will come and bail them out. In the absence of district policy for school renewal, superintendents and boards, knowingly or not, leave themselves totally open to pressure groups. The politically expedient thing to do is to make up policy as one goes along, according to who is screaming the loudest. The moral thing to do is to develop policies that will promote the core goal of education and congruent principles of teaching and learning that allow schools to stay the course.

Chapter Nine

Common Dilemmas of Good Schools

For schools to fulfill their central mission of preparing students for productive citizenship in a democratic society, they themselves must operate in a democratic fashion around their core beliefs about teaching and learning. Such a dramatic shift away from how most public schools traditionally have operated will take time. To flourish, democracies must be built from within, must develop parameters for their actions, and must be concerned foremost about their present and future citizens (in a school's case, the education of their students).

Democracies, by definition, are not clean, efficient, harmonious organizations, predicated on simple external answers. Rather, they flourish on ideological conflict, disequilibrium, and internally developed answers. The demarcation between successful and unsuccessful democracies is that the successful ones focus on defining the good of all, engage in critical study of what actions might work, create a willingness of people to put their differences aside (at least temporarily) in order to reach collective decisions and mobilize for the common good, and act thoughtfully, with continuous study and revision. Unsuccessful democracies become mired in divisiveness, bureaucratization, and anarchy. Indeed, these distinctions between successful and unsuccessful democracies are identical to distinctions between schools that work powerfully for students and those that flounder or remain ineptly the same.

131

If schools continue to operate by mandates and external prescriptions (whereby the omniscient local "boss" and centralized authorities lead the workers around), and smoothness, efficiency, and compliance are of greater value than the moral aspirations of a community, then we will be left with what we have now—the impossibility of the public school to realize its essential focus. Students cannot learn to live in a democracy and think critically, creatively, and self-reliantly when their school environment stifles such values among adults. The failure of public education has been its inability to come to grips with the hypocrisy of espousing democracy, with all the accompanying rhetoric (about character education, civics, values education, students as active workers, cooperative learning) while being antidemocratic in the spirit and action of its own organization. The ultimate challenge of public school education is to return to its reason for being.

Public education, with all the various interests pushed upon it, has forgotten why a democracy has public schools. Jerome Bruner, the eminent educator, once said that education is an endeavor of learning how to manage dilemmas, rather than how to solve problems. Those who live or work in the day-to-day life of schools know what he meant. Problems, once identified or properly diagnosed, have solutions that can be applied, and then the problems are gone. Dilemmas, by contrast, are troublesome situations of tension, trade-offs, and competing consequences, no matter what the solution. School renewal is not a straight line of solving one problem after another, until all the hurdles are crossed and the finish line is reached. Educational renewal means managing a stream of predicaments and learning to live with competing consequences, so that, over time, the school comes closer to realizing its goals for students.

As we saw in the previous chapter, if a school takes the initiative in school renewal, it is most likely to increase conflict among participants and receive additional criticism from outsiders. Thus, in solving one problem—becoming more democratic—the school creates two additional ones: internal conflict, and external scorn. What seemed at first glance like the solution to a problem is really a dilemma; one apparent solution creates further tension to be resolved. This is life in a self-renewing school. To believe that a purposeful and moral school can operate without dilemmas and tension, and that a finished state of utopia can be reached, is delusionary, at least, if not downright psychotic. A good school is constantly seeking and creating new dilemmas for itself, as part of its own learning process.

Common Dilemmas of Good Schools

Time

On hundreds of occasions, when I have spoken to members of individual schools and districts about school renewal, the question of time has been brought up. How can a school become self-renewing, have a covenant and a charter, engage in critical study, and take control of educational tasks without spending enormous amounts of faculty, staff, and administrative time in meetings? How is the school to continue dealing with the day-to-day matters of classroom teaching, students' needs, parents' concerns, building and grounds maintenance, paperwork, and all the other demands while beginning or implementing a democratic process of school renewal?

There is no single clear solution. A few commonsense ideas, from rudimentary to complex ones, will be suggested here in the form of questions.

1. Could existing planning days, as well as existing faculty meetings, be reconstructed to offer more time for planning in school renewal?
2. Is there a way of acquiring additional planning time for some members by rescheduling the school day, so that there can be occasional early-release time for the governing council or a task force?
3. Could existing money for staff development be used for school retreats or special planning sessions? Could additional money for planning be sought from the district, the state, or granting agencies?
4. Could or should stipends be given to school community

members who have extraordinary responsibilities for the governance process? For example, some schools routinely give stipends to members involved in extracurricular activities. Could the same be done for the chairperson of the school council or for some other positions?

5. Is there an existing planning process, required by the district, the state, or an accrediting agency, that has to be conducted anyway and could become part of planning for the covenant, the charter, and the critical-study process?

A school must strike a balance between the time people are willing to give to a schoolwide democratic process and the time individuals must devote to their classrooms, families, and personal affairs. For example, dedicated teachers typically want to participate in school renewal, but they do not want to be absent from their classrooms for long periods. Even if the time is used for planning ways of better education for all children, each day away from the classroom is a day lost forever to one's own students. The basic solution to the issue of time is not to solve it. Instead, school community members themselves must be able to decide how much time can be realistically and willingly devoted to this process and what can be done within that time—the greatest priorities within the given time. There are no set solutions. Experience with many schools shows that some find much time, and others move ahead slowly, with less time allocated. The point, for any school, is to get started and then adjust expenditures of time as the years unfold, increasing or decreasing the time according to the will of the community. A shortage of time should never be an excuse for doing nothing.

External Regulations

Policies must be developed that invite willing schools to move beyond existing regulations, within clear parameters, and that keep regulations temporarily in place for schools not yet ready to initiate their own schoolwide changes. Some schools and districts may be ready to go beyond current regulations, but higher authorities are not ready to rethink them. After more than a decade of "legislated learning," most schools and districts are still subjected to uniform regulations of student assessment, curriculum, teacher evaluation, and more. It is also not uncommon to find local schools tightly controlled by uniform requirements of their own districts that are more restrictive than state and federal decrees.[1] For schools and districts ready for democratic self-renewal but caught in a web of top-down regulations, the following guidance may prove helpful:

1. Study existing regulations, and determine which ones are actually helpful or at least will not get in the way.

2. Identify any regulations that truly are immediate barriers. Keep in mind what the school could still do even if the regulations did not change. For example, if the student testing program or the graduation requirements cannot be changed, what other student assessments or activities for graduation could still be performed in a way that would help achieve the primary school goal? A school should not let existing regulations be a reason for not taking at least some self-initiated steps.

3. If an invitational policy for seeking waivers from district or state regulations does not exist, initiate your own requests for waivers. Target the precise regulations standing in the way and prepare a short letter of inquiry, a paper, or an oral presentation to the appropriate authority. A school should have done its homework in making a request, which will state the goal, the intended results, the desired operations (after a review of literature and research), and the needed waiver. The request should have endorsements indicating wide school community support.

4. Press for the development of new policies at the district, state, and federal levels to encourage and invite site-based autonomy. Fortunately, several states now have developed such policies, which could serve as models. The problem with most of them, however, is that they still restrict the number of schools that can be deregulated, and they use past achievement as a major criterion for acceptance. (See Appendix D for an example of a state invitational policy for all schools.)

Individual schools usually have the capacity to move more quickly in making internal changes than external authorities can in responding. When a school wants to initiate, but district or state has no policy or known procedure for giving waivers to schools, tension is the result. A school cannot simply wait, immobilized, but it also cannot simply act on its own, in a manner that is in clear noncompliance with district and state regulations. In such circumstances, during the transition prior to articulation of a new district policy, a school needs to ask openly for external approval. If that is not forthcoming, the school still needs to press ahead with internal change that stays within the letter of the law but finds enough flexibility for the school to act consistently with its principles. This is a tough dilemma that can be resolved in the future. For now, it must be discussed openly, and communication must be kept flowing among initiating schools, the district, and the state.

Voice

Voice means influence and control over decisions. The school-based renewal movement should not exclude representatives of teachers' unions and associations, district officials, superintendents, school board members, business or civic groups, and others from matters of educational practice at the school level. Nevertheless, school renewal should rest squarely on the shoulders of those closest to teaching and learning — teachers, school-based administrators, staff, parents, and students themselves. Within this circle, what groups should have the greatest representation and voice in decision making? There must be a clear rationale for why one group should have a greater voice than others.

I recently attended a meeting of various task forces dealing with how to improve an entire community in one of the highest-poverty and highest-crime areas of a large city. The participants were there to decide on ways to improve education, safety, employment, housing, and the general health and well-being. Local citizens comprised the majority of the participants, but there were also officials from hospitals, banks, the police department, social service agencies, public schools, and others. It was clear that those officials, although they were *involved* in the community, were not *residents* of the community. They were there to provide information, insight, and suggestions and, most of all, to listen and respond to the needs of the residents. The residents were to have the majority influence in final decisions because no one knew better than the residents themselves what happens to them. This meeting, one in a series of meetings throughout high-poverty areas of this city, was an example of democracy at the local level, in the tradition of the old town meetings.

In a school community, the residents who live most intimately with the issues of schoolwide teaching and learning are teachers. Similarly, these "residents" should have the majority voice in those decisions. The principal should be a key participant. Parents and caretakers, students, paraprofessionals, district personnel, and civic or business leaders should be active members. District officials, however, should serve in a role similar to that of the officials at the urban meeting: they should be resource people offering information, ideas, suggestions, and inside expertise on linking resources to the needs and ideas of residents developing programs.

This idea is sure to alienate some, but district officials, teachers' union or association representatives, parents, school administrators, and other groups should not have the majority influence or veto over decisions about teaching and learning in an individual school. Parents should have the majority say in parental matters. District officials should have the majority say in district matters. Teachers should have the majority say in teaching matters. There are two reasons why. One reason is obvious, and one is less so. The first reason is that decisions about teaching and learning affect teachers the most; they, more than anyone else in a school or district, must live with the consequences of those decisions in their day-to-day lives. The second reason is that teachers know more about teaching, potential changes, and likely consequences for students than anyone else does. Teachers should have more say about schoolwide teaching matters than anyone else because *they have not left teaching*.

People who have become principals, union representatives, central office supervisors, or superintendents have given up their "residency" in the teaching community by leaving the classroom. This does not mean that such people and positions cannot be valuable participants and have a voice, but it does mean that they should not have majority control over local school decisions.

For school renewal to sustain itself, teaching has to come of age as a profession, and current assumptions about teachers and their influence on teaching matters must be reversed. It is ordinary for teachers to leave teaching and become principals, curriculum directors, superintendents, or union heads in order to have greater influence in education, or to have the time to make changes that cannot be made by teachers. The absurdity and wrongness of this thinking holds schools back from realizing their potential. Why must teachers leave teaching in order to have a voice in changing teaching? Why should the benefits of time, flexibility, communication, visits with others, and (usually) higher salary accrue to those who leave teaching? Let me be blunt: the reason why teachers do not have more time, more flexibility, and more opportunities for professional dialogue is that our current system gives those benefits to people who leave teaching, rather than allocating those benefits to those who stay. If this mentality is not reversed, teaching will never be the attractive profession it should be. Schools will never sustain school renewal until those who stay in teaching are rewarded by having the greatest influence over what happens in teaching and learning, and until those who leave teaching serve primarily as resources for teachers and their decisions. If you leave teaching, you lose your right to be a primary voice. This is a tough premise to swallow, and much ego, status, and power are at stake in keeping things the way they are, but a profession cannot exist in schools where teachers do not have the greatest say about the core work of teaching.

Such a change in dismantling hierarchies and dependency relations has occurred in some schools, has begun in others, and is being thought about in others, but this change will not come about if decentralizing initiatives to schools simply replace one level of management with another. Site-based schools run by lay citizens, management teams of administrators, appointed grade-level or departmental heads, or single principals are not the answer to self-renewal. Developmentally, teachers and administrators may not yet be willing to distribute, share, and take these responsibilities, and transitional stages toward democracy may be appropriate, but the end is clear.

Majority representation by teachers in decisions about teaching does not imply that a teacher alone should have a greater vote than any other school community member. To make good decisions for students, all members of the school community should be involved. The solution to the dilemma of voice has to do with where to begin with one's covenant, charter, and critical-study process and whether to have all groups represented at once or to begin mainly with educators (teachers and administrators) and then expand representation of parents, students, and others over time.

Coordinating with Other Schools

It is possible to construe site-based democratic school renewal as the unleashing of a hodge-podge of individual school initiatives that have no relation to what other schools in the same district or state are doing. The development of state and district invitational policies may be seen as creating an anarchy of individual school efforts. Exactly the opposite will occur, however, if districts and states provide support and link schools to one another. After the initial flurry of piloting efforts, there will be greater coordination of school efforts in implementation than now occurs under highly centralized and explicitly uniform regulations. The difference is that coordination will spring from the bottom up—from the interest of school people in learning from one another, and from the efforts of school people to ensure continuity of educational practice for their students as they move from school to school.

We have become so accustomed to thinking that the coordination of curricula, instructional programs, and assessment happens only by centralized fiat that we have forgotten that most successful coordination comes from people who want to discover ways of improving their practice by learning from and sharing with each other. For example, is cooperative learning, as an instructional practice, or the learning portfolio, as an assessment practice, better coordinated by a district or a state that determines the need, develops the idea, sets up training for schools, establishes schedules, provides training, and sends out monitors to assess the implementation? Or is it better coordinated and sustained when individual schools, through their own governance processes, decide on a need and join with like-minded schools in the district or state to work with resource people and learn to implement the effort jointly? Schools in comparable settings or spans of grade levels, using the critical-study dimension of the three-dimensional framework, may well be exploring some of the same changes; they will not want to reinvent the wheel. This may sound paradoxical, but it would be perfectly appropriate for schools to participate in district- or state-coordinated staff development programs, curriculum work, and other teaching-related practices when a need has arisen in multiple schools.

Does anyone truly believe that only district or state officials care that what a student learns in one school not be eradicated at the next level of schooling? Most primary, elementary, middle, and secondary school educators—on their own, and without prodding—care very much about what happens to their students. The dilemma in decentralized activities is how to coordinate the groundswell of individual school concern and save every school from the need to work and invent alone.

Schools that share students across levels will naturally want to know (and coordinate, to some degree) what they are doing. Coordination does not imply sameness of programs, but it does mean that each school understands the educational experiences and assessments provided by the others enough that it can build on them and prepare students for the next level. Again, this is where district personnel can serve another need, providing opportunities for schools to meet and be better informed about and coordinated with one another's work.

Dependence on External Authorities

Knowingly or not, commercial publishers, staff development consultants and trainers, and district and state officials have formed an alliance that has repeatedly diminished the ability of local educators to think critically and responsibly. The marketing of answers for schools has kept schools habitually dependent on external authorities. Layers of centralized positions, highly expensive consultants and educational programs, teacher and school effectiveness programs, commercial books, textbooks, and kits have claimed to virtually guarantee improved student learning and performance. This multimillion-dollar industry has generated high volumes of articles, presentations, books, and workshops, which produce an endless list of factors, components, dimensions, and elements that schools need, in the proper way, to be successful.[2]

I do not want to suggest that there is a secret and conscious conspiracy of publishers, staff developers, consultants, and researchers meeting late at night and plotting to keep local educators dependent. Most of these people, like the rest of us, have good intentions to be helpful, but what they are doing, in their own advocacy of answers for others, is continuing the separation of teachers from decisions about teaching and diminishing the democratic capacity of a school for knowledge production and knowledge application.

More often, school improvement or "restructuring" is done by states or districts. They "go shopping" to find the best-sounding innovation, program, or consultant and show local school people what to do. Members of the local school community are made to believe, or have internalized the belief, that educational change is the province of others.

I will never forget the principal of a fine middle school who called and asked me to recommend a consultant to conduct a year-long series of workshops on a literacy-based curriculum. Knowing the middle school, I was startled by her request. The school had three teachers with great expertise in this approach, and their classes were recognized as exemplary models of practice. I asked the principal whether the task force on staff development had thought of using the school's own faculty for the workshops. She paused and said, "No, it never occurred to us or to me to use our own. We just thought an outside expert would be better." In my question, the principal's pause, and the later deliberation of the task force, people in the school realized how often they had denied their own expertise and saw how they could acquire knowledge without relying on external authority. This scenario is not atypical of many schools.

No external educational authority — no matter how renowned or well researched — knows for sure what others should do. At best, what such persons or programs can do, if they are honest, is say what they think will work, under what conditions, on the basis of their own experiences. External programs, materials, consultants, and research can and should be considered and possibly used when a school makes its own decisions, but a school should look first for resources within. Only when there is no internal expertise or no obvious way to help people acquire it should a school look outside.

Sequence, Emphasis, and Pace of Educational Change

Books are written sequentially — from left to right, in numbered chapters. The problem with such sequential arrangement is that it flies in the face of reality. School renewal is not sequential. Factors of readiness and different intervention points must be taken into account. For example, some sides of the three-dimensional framework, and some educational tasks within the framework, are easier to build than others. At one school, it may be better to develop the covenant before the charter. At another, it may be better to develop the critical-study process before the covenant. At another school, it may be more appropriate to develop the charter and then develop the covenant and critical-study process from it. At still another school, it may be best to do all three tasks at once.

Schools have different histories and constellations of people and personalities. Developing the covenant at one school may be so boring that it deflates enthusiasm for further schoolwide work.

Or a school may recently have written a mission statement for some requirement, which was felt to be a waste of time, and the covenant may seem suspiciously similar. In such a school, one of the two other sides of the framework may spark more interest and willingness. In another school, however, creating the covenant may be a highly energizing and satisfying endeavor that gives momentum to the building of the other two sides. This school may be a congenial one whose community has never tackled a collegial task of this magnitude, and it sounds exciting. Members may think that it makes sense to have everyone come together, talk across grades and departments, and, for the first time, try to figure out what learning should be about.

To sustain educational renewal, it is critical for a school to have the three-dimensional framework, but it need not be built in a particular order.

The same holds true for the sequence of educational tasks. *Some educational tasks — the work of internal change — are more accessible to planning and implementation than others* (see Chapter Five). These tasks are what a school has under its control and can adjust, modify, or change in order to reach its core goal.

Which tasks to work on first, and the order of working on them, cannot be prescribed externally. One school may already have implemented top-quality site-based staff development programs and may now wish to integrate that work into a new coaching process among teachers and administrators. Another school may be timid in trying to bring about instructional change through schoolwide staff development and coaching. A school's history of isolation and suspicion may make the idea of teachers' opening their classroom doors to one another for observation and feedback too threatening; a more comfortable launching pad for collegial work may be curriculum development or the instructional budget. In developing plans for what should be taught and what materials should be purchased to support a new curriculum, people may come together more easily. They can then get to know each other better before addressing some of the other educational tasks.

Ideally, decisions about which tasks should be given greater emphasis, and when, should follow from schoolwide

learning priorities. Which task, if changed, has the greatest like-
lihood to improve identified conditions for students? To take on
a task that already has negative associations may set a school
back, whereas it can move ahead on the realization of its priorities if, in the beginning, it takes on tasks that it feels neutral
about, open to, or fairly comfortable with.

It would be heavenly if school renewal were as easy as
textbooks, illustrations, and diagrams suggest. Fortunately, the
process does not lend itself to prescriptions that override the individual context of the school. Knowing where to enter and what
pace to assume is itself a process of making educated decisions
about what is most likely to work now and lead to better work
later on. A school discovers whether it has responded appropri-
ately to this dilemma by taking action, studying the action, and
determining whether the work is bringing the school together
in achieving educational results for students. If it is not, the entry
point may have been a mistake, and the school will have to
rethink entry points, emphases, and tasks for the next round.

Dysfunctional Behavior

What if a school does everything suggested in this book? Do
the resisters, the complainers, the apathetic, and the whiners
just suddenly become involved, enthused, committed, and wise?
There will always be people who do not like or do not want to
be involved, and who will try their hardest to subvert and squash
the plans of a school. Such people exist right now in schools
that are conventional, bureaucratic, hierarchical, and authoritarian, and they will exist in schools that are collegial, flexible, par-
ticipatory, and democratic. They come from all positions, all
experience levels, and all backgrounds. The pragmatic issue is
not whether they exist but rather in which type of school will
there be less dysfunctional behavior, and in which type of school
there will be more pressure on dysfunctional people to "get with
the program."

Over time, in truly democratic schools, there will be fewer
dysfunctional persons than in nondemocratic schools. In schools
where there is a push to include, listen to, and invite people

to participate, there will be less apathy and fewer complaints. It will not happen overnight. It may take several years for people to believe that they really can make an equal contribution (or to choose not to). Truly democratic schools, by definition, will have more people contributing and less dysfunctional behavior because the responsibility for turning the behavior around rests with the entire school community rather than with one person in authority. Therefore, the pressure to change dysfunctional behavior is greater and more persuasive in democratic schools. A person who exhibits dysfunctional behavior, and the school community members who are the targets, spark a two-way responsibility for change.

In conventional schools, the dysfunctional behavior of a school member is mainly an issue between the principal, who is responsible for the actions of his employees, and the dysfunctional person. The rest of the school members, besides rolling their eyes and exchanging the latest gossip about the battle going on between the two parties, mostly stay out of the issue. If they do feel a need to take sides, they tend to side with their colleague, rather than with the principal. But even taking sides usually means not helping the administration try to correct the problem.[3]

In a democratic school, when a member is dysfunctional, he or she is out of compliance with what the school community has determined to be in the best interest of students and in accord with the school's covenant for teaching and learning. Therefore, dysfunctional behavior is seen as going against the norms of the school community, rather than against the expectations of an employer. The dysfunctional person is interfering with what the school is trying to accomplish, and the school community needs to figure out how to correct the situation. When the school accepts the choice to act as a community, it also accepts responsibility for supervising itself and not passing such problems on to authority figures.

School community members need to be sensitive to the fact that complaining and resisting are normal human symptoms of feeling excluded or of not believing that one has been listened to or of believing that what is being done is not the right thing to do. All members, at some time, have exhibited the same dysfunctional behavior that they are seeing in someone who is obstructing the school's work. Therefore, the first step toward resolution is to analyze why one would act in the same way — in what circumstances, and for what reasons. Instead of seeing the behavior as symptomatic of the person's dysfunction, see it as a reflection of how the person has been included, communicated with, and treated by the group. For example, if dysfunctional behavior is characteristic of a small percentage of school members, it may be a signal that the school needs to work harder in learning how to listen and to include rather than finding out ways to ignore, exclude, or blame the dysfunctional members.

Only by such reflective action can a school community determine whether the dysfunctional behavior is a result of poor involvement and communication or of lack of belief in what the school has decided to do. (Words that suggest a values-based stance of opposition are usually cast in the first person: "I am not going to change my teaching that way. I don't care what anyone else thinks, I'm not going to do it.")

If it becomes apparent that the dysfunctional behavior is values-based, then the next issue of democratic management kicks in: how to respect an individual's rights and still move forward as a school. If it acts too hastily, a community that has not weighed the opposition's views carefully may disregard important information. Expressions of disagreement are to be valued in the decision-making process, and the school should give all members ample opportunity to make the opposing case.

If push comes to shove, however, after the school community has listened, tried to be inclusive, considered alternatives, and deliberately made a schoolwide decision consistent with its covenant and its decision-making process, then confrontation is inevitable. This is the hardest part of collective responsibility: a community must tell its own members that something was agreed upon and is going to be done. Reluctant people can ask for help with accepting the implementation, but no one individual or group of individuals can stop what the group has legitimately decided.

This does not mean that a decision or a plan cannot be

reconsidered later, after a trial period. Critical study of actions is part of the process. Nevertheless, a member either must act as part of the school or must face the consequences. On several occasions, I have heard school community members confront their colleagues in words to this effect: "We want you here. You are entitled to your beliefs and expressions. But if you cannot accept the decision, then we would like you to consider taking a different position, where you will not be an obstacle to the work." These words are not easy and not nice. Many times they are avoidable, but the world is not perfect. Dysfunctional behavior is the responsibility of everyone in a democratic school.

Dilemmas and Decisions

These dilemmas suggest that school renewal is always an educational process of making informed judgments about competing alternatives. The fact that there is no science or exact technology for school renewal reaffirms the central importance of analysis, insight, reason, and passion in the core work of education. If there is ever absolute precision in this work, then education as a process of thinking will have been lost, and there will be no reason for the existence of schools or democracies.

Chapter Ten

Conclusion:
Staying the Course

You got to look at things with the eye in your heart, not with the eye in your head.
Lame Deer
(cited by Crow Dog and Erdoes, 1990)

A young child responded to her grandfather's request to describe the world. She said, "It is made up of grass, trees, sky, and clouds." The child squinched her brow, thought further, and then looked squarely at her grandfather and said, "I think I left out a thing or two."[1] I have probably left out more than a thing or two about school renewal, but my instinct is to end the book with this chapter.

I have not touched on several other important areas of public education, including teacher education and leadership preparation programs, teacher recruitment and retention, and certification and licensing of professionals. I have also omitted such broader issues of public education as preschool programs, early infancy interventions, adult literacy and continuing education, and prenatal and parenting programs. The broad coordination of "seamless" education from birth to death, based on democratic principles and goals, has critical merit for discussing, planning, and implementing. The expanse that I have focused on, however, is our public schools, which millions of our youngsters attend, and which a sizable proportion of our local and state taxes supports.

What has been proposed in this book is that our public schools, in order to sustain themselves, will need to refocus their goal on the very reason for their creation: to prepare citizens for productive participation in a democracy. Our schools, the rhetoric notwithstanding, are no worse than before and, in some cases, are much better. The problem with our schools is not that students are dropping out (at lower percentages than in years past), or that they are not first in international comparisons on mathematics or science tests, or that their performance is the cause of the nation's economic woes. Rather, the failure of our schools is that our students have become increasingly disengaged and alienated from participation as members of their larger society. In most of our schools, learning has little relevance to becoming a citizen. Our students are not learning the essentials — how to care about, know about, and act for the betterment of the larger community. Education and democracy are conditioned on one another; the mixture gives energy to drive a more enlightened and decent society.

For a true awakening of our schools, we must return to their central goal: democratic participation. Other areas of achievement (in reading, writing, mathematics, art, and music) are more fully learned when they are viewed as subsets of student involvement in the core issues of local and expanded communities.

To rejuvenate education, the public school itself must become a model of thoughtful and moral discourse. It does so by building and operating the three-dimensional framework. The first side is the covenant: the agreed-upon principles of teaching and learning that the school community pledges to promote. The second side is the charter: the agreed-upon and explicitly democratic process by which school community members acquire genuine power in making educational decisions. The third side is the critical-study process, by which the school community gathers information and studies itself as it strives to achieve learning priorities.

With the three-dimensional framework in place, the school community is ready to do the work of educational rejuvenation. That work includes such elements as schoolwide curriculum development, staff development, coaching, instructional programs, learning assessment, instructional materials, staffing, and scheduling. Over time, the school must determine a pace and a scope for change that will make it a qualitatively better place than before.

District and state policies must change, to support the primary goal of public education and respect the developmental differences of schools. Such policies must not mandate uniformity and procedures. Rather, they must view fairness as enabling equality of accomplishment, not sameness of educational treatment. Policies must invite the school to move beyond existing regulations and use a site-based covenant, a charter, and a critical-study process to craft a unique, powerful educational environment. If schools stay within the givens of constitutional law, equity, multicultural sensitivity, attention to research, progress toward achievement of learning goals, and public disclosure of results, then they should be actively encouraged to be as creative and imaginative as possible. The role of districts, boards, and state agencies becomes one of supporting schools by decentralizing resources, linking schools, providing technical and human assistance, and keeping access open to schools that are not yet ready to initiate school renewal.

An awakening of schools, districts, and states to the central democratic goal of schools will create confusion, controversy, and dilemmas — in sum, the peaks and valleys characteristic of emerging, free, moral communities. Such tensions should be expected, and clear policies for schools will serve as a stabilizer for the stormy weather ahead. In the end, what will have been achieved will be a school reform movement that will endure because it will have a foundation not easily buffeted by fads, innovations, and shifting political winds. It will be secure as a true democracy is secure — in its constant openness and its inquiry into the larger questions of society. Renewal will endure, not because it will attain role maintenance, but rather because it will constantly be challenged. More thought, more study, more participation, and more action will be demanded.

This surely is not a perfect world, but it is a more moral world than we have now in our schools and in our society. School community members will not become wise, knowing, and effective all at once. A community has to learn as it goes — to learn from successes and, just as important, to learn from failures and crises. In a true community, wisdom is built over time and is based on cumulative experience. So it will be in the rejuvenation of the public schools.

Are schools, districts, states, and teacher associations ready for such a challenge? Some are already in the midst of it, and many more would like the opportunity to participate. Those not wishing or not ready to learn can sit temporarily on the sidelines and follow existing regulations and structures enforced by districts and states. But old notions of control, influence, power, and status will have to go, and this will be hard to learn. For those ready to learn and initiate, the time is now. Together, they can create a tidal wave of enduring school renewal. As Barber (1992, p. 65) has written, "Democracy grows from the bottom up and cannot be imposed from the top down. Civil society has to be built from the inside out . . . . There is always a desire for self-government, always some expression of participation, consent, and representation in traditional hierarchies. These need to be identified, tapped, modified, and incorporated into new democratic procedures."

Restructuring Policy

We must rethink policies for school change — invitations to willing schools; venture capital; structures for schools and districts that are not ready; boards and state agencies as coordinators of the work of individual schools, rather than as enforcers of uniform compliance. Those who have previously controlled schools, teachers, and teaching — districts, states, school boards, teacher unions, universities, consultants, and commercial publishers — will have to restructure themselves. Little in education and schools will change if those who have traditionally exercised control over teaching, teachers, and schools do not accept this premise: those who leave the local school community lose the right to exercise dominative influence over decisions at the local site. If one has chosen to become a superintendent, a central office person, a university faculty member, or a board member, then one has intentionally removed oneself from the web of the local school community. The job of one who has left is to help those who have stayed and provide the time, resources, and assistance to judge for themselves what has to be done. The people who have stayed behind must learn to lead; those who have left must learn to follow.

That is why we must stop thinking about *national* reform as a way of improving schools. The tradition of vesting authority for educational policies in external agencies, far removed from individual schools, must end. State commissions, governors' offices, national commissions, and national associations have served more to distract schools from their moral work than to help mobilize them in ways that will best help students learn. The only reforms that mean much are *local* reforms, in *local* schools and *local* communities. Local school community members have spent too much time reacting to state and national reports and external regulations and too little time developing their own ideas for their schools. We need to find more time for school communities to study themselves and get to work. Then and only then will we have an enduring national reform movement. The only national reform that will make much sense is a national reform made up of local reforms in the aggregate.

A Sobering Appraisal

This book deals directly with the essential work of schools, but other influences that affect education are not under the primary control of local school communities. For example, there are dilapidated school buildings unfit for human occupancy, with inadequate heating and cooling systems, structural flaws, poor lighting, and general lack of maintenance. Drugs and violence in the outer community bring gangs, muggings, theft, and extortion into the schools. There are inadequate services for children living with little adult supervision and with few means of experiencing museums, libraries, and other institutions of historical, cultural, and aesthetic value. The list could go on to include teenage pregnancy, poor prenatal care, inadequate health care, and much more.

Our public schools contribute only a piece of what influences and educates students: the internal work of education;

only indirectly does it deal with the external work of improving conditions in society.

This distinction sets realistic limits on what a school community can do and helps to define the role of the other agencies and organizations that the school must collaborate with.

I shall direct the following statements primarily to educators in schools (principals, teachers, and paraprofessionals) and secondarily to other members of the school community (parents, caretakers, business and civic leaders, and other citizens):

1. The primary work of a public school community is to enhance the quality of teaching and learning within the school and to forge links to student learning outside the school.
2. The primary work of a public school community is not to spend time planning with respect to poverty, crime, health, social services, housing, and welfare.
3. The primary work of a public school community is a piece of the larger work of enhancing the total quality of a child's life.

Now, after stating this, I cringe at how it might be interpreted. Am I saying that a school community should be indifferent to these other issues? Not at all. I am saying that until schools understand the locus of control of *their own* responsibilities — teaching and learning — they will spend their time figuring out what *other* agencies should be doing and will forget or ignore what they themselves should be doing and why there are schools in the first place. To put this another way, teachers should not be spending most of their time planning lunch programs, maintaining their buildings, planning prenatal parenting programs, or providing additional psychological or social services. They should be spending most of their professional time discussing and planning for teaching and learning.[2] It is up to others in the school community to determine connections with other agencies, to coordinate a wider spectrum of educational services. In the case of schools with deplorable physical conditions and striking inequality of resources, it is the moral obligation of districts and states to rectify those conditions.

Some of the most successful schools for impoverished students are strongly coordinated with other community services, but at the center of these schools is a strong covenant for teaching and learning and a sense of the need to stay focused on the internal work of schoolwide educational practice. Some of the worst schools are those where internal practice is neglected, and the onus of responsibility for educating students is shifted to external parties.

What this analysis means is that, for now, school renewal alone will not save our children from the life that they live after school. There will still be hunger, violence, neglect, and unspeakable tragedy. What school renewal will do is take children squarely from these outside conditions and educate them in the most profound, powerful, and purposeful way that a school community can imagine. If all other institutions would do likewise in dealing with their primary responsibilities and then link up with one another, we would have integrative care for our children, our communities, and our society at large. The total challenge is daunting, but to begin is to begin with oneself. If public education can engender in students a desire to participate as productive citizens in the larger society, then we will indeed have a better place for future generations.

Believing

Schools, districts, and states that take up the challenge of creating local school renewal will find that day-to-day realities will continue to crop up and make immediate life unpredictable — sometimes crazy, always interesting. Influence outside the school will continue to seep in. Problems with logistics and schedules will continue. In the course of thousands of human interactions each day, some will be problematic. In the short term, the observable changes in a school beginning renewal may not be obvious. Classrooms, the curriculum, grouping, and teaching may appear to be only somewhat modified, and students may not seem much more productive, excited, or involved than before. School renewal is not a day-to-day proposition. It is a long-term, continuous proposition, and commitment must be for the long term.

In many cases, schools can expect to achieve modest improvements for students in the first year of renewal and will see more comprehensive and dramatic changes after three, four, or five years. These schools move to a rhythm of surges and lulls. At times, maintaining change is paramount. At other times, discarding existing routines is paramount. At all times, however, there is a clear purpose and direction to the work.

The ultimate issue is staying the course — *believing* that the work of a democratic school will benefit students and, eventually, society at large. The actions taken may not always be correct, but when results are not forthcoming, the school needs to alter its decisions and actions, not its belief in democratic principles. In this way, democracy in its three-dimensional educational framework — the covenant, the charter, and the critical analysis — transcends the setbacks, crises, and transitions of community members. Democracy reflects a belief in how a community and the larger society should operate to protect individual lives and enhance the community. To paraphrase Thomas Jefferson, when citizens in a democracy make an unwise decision, the solution is not to abandon democracy, but rather to learn from the decision so as to make wiser decisions in the future.

Democracy as a core belief transcends empirical argument. Rational analysis can proceed, data can accumulate, and thoughtful logic can apply. In the end, however, there is no universal proof that democratic societies produce better mathematicians, less crime, or fewer people in hunger than undemocratic societies do. What the belief in democracy does is to ensure that the issues of our society are issues that citizens care about, participate in resolving, and take responsibility for. Many democracies are democracies in name only; they do not engender the participation, involvement, and responsibility of their citizens. That is why the role of public education and school renewal is so crucial to the rejuvenation of a more caring, a more enlightened, and a wiser citizenship.

The belief in, rather than the empirical truth about, democracy is the foundation of a society that millions of people throughout the world have given their lives to create, protect, and maintain. We must do the same in our schools. To return to their central mission of preparing democratic citizens, schools must be founded on the same bedrock of belief. We need to strive for the same microcommunity in our schools that we as a people would wish to have as a macrocommunity in our society.

A teacher friend of mine, who works in a renowned democratic school, describes why his school has come so far in the past decade, with documented success in preparing its students: "The reason why our school continues to work is that, as a community, we won't let it *not* work. No matter how frustrated, angry, and impatient we feel at times with each other, we know that we will not stray from our belief about democracy and education. Every challenge will be met because there is no other acceptable way." What he is describing is the cycle built on a reasoned faith that belief in core democratic principles frames the operations and decisions that will produce similar beliefs, operations, and decisions in students. This, in essence, is the challenge of renewing schools. It is time to go to work.

Appendix A

Foxfire Core Practices

1. All the work teachers and students do together must flow from student desires and student concerns.
2. The role of the teacher must be that of collaborator and team leader and guide, rather than boss.
3. The academic integrity of the work must be absolutely clear.
4. The work is characterized by student action, rather than by passive receipt of processed information.
5. A constant feature of the process is its emphasis on peer teaching, small-group work, and teamwork.
6. Connections between the classroom work and surrounding communities and the real world outside the classroom are clear.
7. There must be an audience beyond the teacher for student work.
8. As the year progresses, new activities should spiral gracefully out of the old, incorporating lessons learned from past experiences, building on skills and understandings that can now be amplified.
9. As teachers, we must acknowledge the worth of aesthetic experience, model that attitude in our interactions with students, and resist the momentous policies and practices that deprive students of the chance to use their imaginations.
10. Reflection — some conscious, thoughtful time to stand apart

from the work itself—is an essential activity that must take place at key points throughout the work.

11. The work must include unstintingly honest, ongoing evaluation for skills and content, and changes in student attitude.

Reprinted by permission from *Hands On* ("Foxfire Core Practices," 1991).

Appendix B

Sample Charter of Democratic Governance

This sample charter is a combination of six different charters used by various schools. It should be seen as a simple illustration of the points for a school to consider in developing its own charter, not as a charter to be imitated. There are multiple ways to govern democratically and many entry points. The following example is of governance with broad representation involving students, parents, the community, and the district. Many schools do not begin with such broad representation. Some schools use a final decision rule, going back to all members for approval.

Preamble

It is our shared belief that we should maintain an emphasis on teaching and learning. *Accountability* and *responsibility* are two key words describing our democratic decision-making process. We strive to be open to new ideas and work through consensus or voting to arrive at decisions. Once group decisions are made, we all are expected to support them. Decisions are reevaluated as necessary. It is our continual mission to develop school-renewal activities that meet the needs of all our students, not just for the benefit of one particular group.

Charge

We seek to uphold our school covenant of teaching and learning principles through the following actions:

- To display concern for the total student and the needs of the school as a whole
- To foster an invitational and cooperative learning environment
- To be creative decision makers and problem solvers
- To communicate information systematically
- To develop internal leadership ability
- To be risk takers
- To stay informed
- To continuously evaluate our decisions, activities, and results for students

Composition of the School Council

The council will consist of fourteen voting members. Terms served on the council will be for a period of three years, with four or five positions available for election each year. A council member can succeed himself or herself if reelected. (Exception: The initial council will serve a two-year term before the rotation process begins. Vacancies on the council are to be filled for unexpired terms by elected members from representative groups.)

> Administrative staff (principal): one standing member
> Classroom teachers, counselors, and specialists: seven elected members
> Representatives of parent organization: two elected members
> Representative of student organization: one elected member
> Community/business partner: one elected member
> Other school staff personnel: two elected members
> District consultant: member ex officio

The school council will be responsible for the following tasks:

- Gathering information and ideas from all faculty, through the communication groups
- Establishing priorities for schoolwide improvements and organizing special task forces

- Making decisions on recommendations from the task forces
- Collecting and evaluating evidence of schoolwide improvement

Communication groups will consist of certified and noncertified staff members randomly allocated to each group. Each communication group will be led by an elected member of the council. Groups will meet monthly with their council representatives to disseminate information and to discuss concerns and ideas for schoolwide improvements. The parent and student representatives will use the parent and student organizations as their communication groups. Changes in the formation and assignment of members in communication groups will be made as members of the council change.

Special task forces will be formed on the basis of schoolwide concerns for school renewal. Each task force chairperson (not a council member) will be responsible for making progress reports and recommendations in writing to the council. A recorder will be selected to take minutes of each meeting. Minutes will be given to the vice chairperson of the council, who will serve as the liaison between the council and the task forces.

Standing committees will be determined by the council to deal primarily with nonteaching and nonlearning matters (student discipline, extracurricular activities, building maintenance, fundraising, coordination of social services). The composition of the committees will reflect representation of those most affected by the matters under discussion. Membership will include staff, parents, students, and community leaders.

Limitations of Groups

The responsibilities of the school council and of school governance will be specific, will address schoolwide issues, and will focus on educational areas in need of improvement. The following areas will be restricted from consideration:

- Systemwide issues
- Personal or individual issues
- Issues in the realm of normal operational or organizational

procedures (administrative or instructional) until a need for improvement has been identified by a communication group
- Issues at variance with established policies of local and state boards of education and other outside governing agencies

The focus will be on what we as a school community should do to better educate all our students.

Meeting Schedules

The school council will meet at least once a month, and more often if necessary. For the purpose of decision making, eight members will be considered a quorum.

Communication groups will meet monthly, and more often if necessary.

Task forces will meet for the first time as scheduled by the vice chairperson of the council. After the initial meeting, they will determine their own schedule of meetings, based on convenient times for members and the number of meetings deemed necessary to accomplish the group's specific task.

Standing committees will determine their own schedule for meetings, normally at least once a quarter. All meetings are open to all members of the school community.

Decision-Making Procedures of the Council

Concerns submitted to the council that are not within the parameters of shared governance will be referred to the appropriate group or individual.

The following procedures have been established for the decision-making process:

1. Task force chairperson submits recommendations in writing to the council.
2. The council reviews, revises, accepts, or rejects the recommendation by consensus. For the purpose of this council, consensus will mean agreement of all members present.
3. If the council does not reach consensus on a decision, representatives return to their communication groups for additional feedback.

4. The council meets a second time, to try to reach consensus.
5. If consensus at the second meeting is still not forthcoming, recommendations are returned to the task force for reevaluation.
6. Recommendations from the task force's chairperson are resubmitted to the council.
7. A two-thirds majority of the council will suffice for a final decision in the event that consensus cannot be reached.
8. If there is not a two-thirds majority, no action is to be taken.

Job Descriptions

Chairperson

Sets agenda for council meetings and schedules meetings
Conducts council meeting by doing the following:
- Stating objective(s) of meeting
- Reviewing agenda
- Outlining procedures for reaching decisions
- Facilitating communication among council members
- Summarizing decisions

Sets agenda for communication group meetings

Vice Chairperson

Assumes duties of chairperson in chairperson's absence
Assists chairperson in planning council meetings if assistance is requested
Assumes duties assigned by chairperson in conducting meetings and making presentations
Serves as the liaison between the council and task forces by doing the following:
- Scheduling the first meeting of the task force
- Supervising the selection of a task force chairperson and recorder
- Providing the recorder with the forms necessary to document task force business
- Scheduling the task force presentation to the council
- Filing task force reports

Recorder

Records decisions reached by council

Records permanent data, such as committee assignments, schedule of next meeting, and so forth

Maintains or arranges maintenance of file containing all council business

Keeps minutes of meetings and circulates to all school community members

Communication Group Leader

Conducts communication group meetings

Gathers and reports information, concerns, and ideas of the group to the council

Informs communication group of activities and decisions of the council

Task Force Chairperson

Sets agendas and conducts task force meetings

Reports on progress of task force to the council

Presents task force recommendations to the council for decision

Task Force Recorder

Takes attendance at task force meetings

Keeps minutes of task force meetings

Completes task force record-keeping forms and gives them to council vice chairperson at conclusion of the task force's work.

Appendix C

The Peakview School Charter

Making a Radical Commitment to Consensus: Decision Making at Peakview

Early in the life of Peakview, when it was still in the conceptual stages, a style or approach to decision making evolved that has become a hallmark of the way we work together. The underlying belief holds that no one person holds all the truth. This basic assumption calls for us to value and respect the wisdom of each member of the staff while continuing to value the insight that we each have gained from our individual experiences and reflection.

In practical terms, it means that:

1. Everyone has the opportunity and responsibility of initiating and then leading the group in the direction of a decision that needs to be made.
2. We all have the responsibility of speaking our minds, so that we all benefit from the thinking of each other, but accepting the responsibility to speak implies accepting the responsibility to listen.
3. When our decisions are based on our collective priorities, we will do our best work, and when time is provided for

This document is used by permission of the Peakview School, in Aurora, Colorado. The process is an adaptation of the Quaker meeting. Some minor adjustments have been made for consistency with the rest of this book.

both discussion and reflection, our decisions will more often be good ones.

We also have become attached to another notion: the distinction between "matters of preference" and "matters of conscience." As in all groups that struggle to do important work, we come to points when differing opinions and even differing philosophies raise the specter of real conflict. At Peakview, we are convinced that on the important issues we will thrive when consensus is reached. However, we have had the experience of reaching for closure on a decision only to find that one or two people remain opposed to the general drift of the large group. It is in those moments that the test of preference versus conscience is applied. If, after careful thought, a dissenting school community member is asked if the personal stand is one of preference, and the answer is yes, then that individual is expected to lay personal preference aside in order to allow the staff to move forward. If, however, the personal stand is a matter of conscience, then the community member assumes that the decision that was in the offing needs either to be delayed or abandoned.

On more than one occasion, we have found agreement and then, upon the reflection of a single member, have had to reopen discussion and undo a decision, so that conscience could be followed. We also have had the experience of having consensus falsely identified, and the next day it has taken the courage of a single member to point out that what was heard was not, in fact, what was said.

As all school communities do, we struggle to find the balance between adequate discussion and thought on an issue and the need to get on with the work of the school through closure of a discussion. We are willing to press ourselves for good decisions, but we also allow and honor the temporary and incomplete decisions that we are sometimes forced to make when we lack the time, energy, or insight to bring a decision to its proper conclusion.

One strategy for decision making that has served us well is the decision to operate as a committee of the whole. Our size (we are a relatively small school) has served us well in this regard. However, even in a relatively small community, this structure, combined with our commitment to real consensus, makes for a decision-making process that is cumbersome and time-consuming, but the corresponding benefits have been clear to us — collectively, we have not made many poor decisions.

While we do not do this perfectly, we value a school culture that allows trust and honesty to prevail in an atmosphere of safety. None of our best efforts at working together would mean much without our fundamental caring for and about one another.

Appendix D

Georgia Schools
for the Future Program:
Invitational Policy

Schools for the Future: Program Guidelines

Introduction

The Georgia Board of Education and the Georgia Department of Education are ushering in a new era through the Schools for the Future program. Schools are encouraged to *restructure local education* to accomplish local, state, and national education goals. The intent of this program is to encourage staff members of individual schools, with the support of local districts, to design the best education programs they can to improve the learning of their own students. It will assist and support schools, districts, and communities in being innovative, creative, and responsible for new approaches to educating students. Local and state rules, regulations, and standards that inhibit proposed restructuring activities will be waived according to the applicable statute.

Demonstration Schools

School restructuring efforts should do the following:

This policy was developed by the Georgia Department of Education, the Georgia Board of Education, and the University of Georgia's Program for School Improvement. The program was modeled on similar policies in Oregon, Washington, British Columbia, and California, and some of the wording is nearly identical. The major difference is the broad scope and unlimited nature of the invitation to all public schools and districts willing to move ahead on internal school renewal.

- Focus on student learning as the end result
- Develop a new conceptualization of learning and teaching
- Engage students in a "thinking curriculum" rich in problem solving, analysis, synthesis, and other thinking skills
- Expect high levels of educational attainment of *all* students
- Focus on learners, not on perpetuating institutions or systems
- Share decision-making authority so that those responsible for carrying out decisions participate in making them
- Address local, state, and national goals

The Schools for the Future program is designed to encourage these tasks:

1. The establishment of measurable goals for educational attainment and high expectations for student performance, including but not limited to improvement in the following performance measures:
   - Student expectations and attitudes about learning
   - Student success in lifelong learning
   - Student attendance rates
   - High school completion rates
   - District, state, and national assessments of student learning and educational progress
   - Parental involvement in school activities
   - Student conduct
2. The restructuring of school organizations, school operations, curriculum, instructional approaches, roles of educators, and formal relationships between and among students, teachers, administrators, parents, and the community, including but not limited to the following modifications:
   - Curriculum
   - Delivery of instruction
   - Assessment of student learning
   - Graduation and promotion requirements
   - Length and structure of the school day and the school year
   - Staffing and formal roles and responsibilities of teachers, administrators, and other school personnel
   - Personnel evaluation and staff development

- State rules, regulations, and standards, as well as local policies related to educational practices
- Formal and informal relationships between school districts and other entities, including community colleges, four-year colleges and universities, businesses, social service agencies, and other institutions

Eligibility

The following schools, with the support of their superintendents and local boards, are eligible to apply under the Schools for the Future program:

1. New schools
2. Existing schools that (a) were in compliance on the most recent evaluation, (b) have previously initiated site-based improvement, and (c) are willing to attempt more creative and responsible educational changes.

Application Procedures

An application must be initiated at the school level. It must be supported by the principal and 85 percent of the teaching staff. The superintendent of schools and the local school board of education must approve the application.

The application process consists of two phases. The school must submit a letter of intent, to be followed by a full application. (For a district that wants to open a new school as a restructured school, the application process should be initiated by the principal of the new school and coordinated with district personnel until the new school is staffed. At this point, the application process will become the responsibility of the principal and staff of the new school.)

Schools may submit letters of intent or applications at any time. Applications will be considered quarterly by the Georgia Board of Education.

Applications may be approved for an initial period of up to three years. All accepted schools will submit yearly evaluations and receive on-site visits. If a school demonstrates success, a three-year renewal of the application may be issued.

The letter of intent should indicate the school's intention to file a full application. The letter should briefly describe what the school staff has done to plan for restructuring, as well as any planning that remains to be done. It should describe the history of the school's involvement in a site-based improvement process, describe the nature of the school's anticipated restructuring, and outline proposed restructuring activities. After the letter has been filed, the applicant will be contacted about whether the proposal is consistent with the intent of the program. The department will help local schools and districts obtain technical assistance to develop their applications.

The application should be developed in a form (written, video, audio, computer-generated, visual, multimedia) and at a length decided by the applicant school. An application cover sheet and a one-page abstract describing the project must be in written form. The application must include the following:

- Identification of the decision-making group, committee, or council in the school and of the shared decision-making procedures for carrying out the overall plan
- The overall goals to be achieved by the restructuring
- The student learning and educational outcomes to be attained
- The major activities of the project, including but not limited to the nature and extent of the restructuring and time lines
- A description of staff development activities required to implement the planned restructuring
- A design for evaluating the effectiveness of the restructuring, including a projection of annual progress on indicators established by the school
- A written statement that district and school administrators are willing to exempt the school from local rules if modification or waiver of local school district rules is required
- Identification of and brief rationale for all state rules, standards, and regulations for which waivers or modifications are requested

- Written statements of support from parents, community agencies, local businesses, and other interested individuals and organizations, if available

Application Review

A Schools for the Future committee will be appointed by the state superintendent of schools. The committee will reflect a balance of local educators (teachers and building and district administrators), local school board members, Department of Education representatives, and others familiar with school renewal and evaluation. These may include college and university faculty, as well as business and community leaders. Committee members will serve on a rotating basis. The Department of Education will provide staff support for the committee.

     The committee will review all letters of intent and all applications and will make recommendations about applications to the state board, through the state superintendent. The state board will consider the recommendations of the committee quarterly and will make final decisions about approval of applications.

Notes

Chapter 1

1. I do not deny that the state has used schools for other purposes, knowingly or not, to sort, rank, and classify children, according to privileged status, to mythologize past wrongs and use schools as labor sources for industry.

2. For a fuller discussion of this point, see Dewey (1940) and Westbrook (1991).

3. I do agree with part of the choice reform agenda. I favor student and parent choice of schools *within* public school districts, provided that (1) all students and parents have equal access to schools, (2) all schools reflect the diverse student population of the district, (3) all public schools are given the opportunity, in terms of finances and support, to develop unique programs, and (4) there is a district strategy to enhance cooperation and collaboration rather than competition among all of its schools (see Chapter Eight for further details). I am adamantly opposed to tuition vouchers that would provide public monies to support private schools. Public schools have an obligation to a democratic mission in the education of students. Private schools, by definition, need not have such an obligation. Many do, but many do not.

Chapter 2

1. I came across these distinctions from listening to and reading the works of Ann Lieberman, Roland Barth, Tom Sergiovanni, Phil Schlechty, and Judith Warren Little. See Barth (1990).
2. In deriving learning principles to fulfill the central goal of public education in a democratic society, it is essential to define the core values of a democracy. We can return to Jefferson and the Declaration of Independence for guidance. Jefferson stressed that a democracy must ensure individual liberty against tyranny and affirm the ideal of human equality (Jefferson, in Padover, 1939). Dewey (1916), likewise, claimed that democracy was more than casting a ballot every four years, but was rather "a mode of associated living . . . of individuals who participate in an interest so that each has to refer his own actions to that of others. . . . " Malcolm X invoked Jefferson to underscore that a democratic society must protect freedom, justice, and equality as well as life, liberty, and the pursuit of happiness for all people (Wilson, 1992). Guttmann (1987) applied this definition of democracy to educational practice and formulated two principles. One principle being nonrepression in that education must not restrict rational deliberations about the good life and society and the other being non-discrimination—that all educable children must be educated.

Chapter 3

1. I am indebted to Lew Allen, who worked with me on this conceptualization.
2. My position, in rule 3, is based on existing organizational roles in schools, not on the future possibilities of different staffing patterns. I am aware that most schools have principals and that they are critical to success. I am further aware that some schools, upon the departure of the principal, spend the money allocated for that position in other ways and do not have a principal per se. In cases where

the decision about resources was aligned with the covenant, these schools are doing fine. All schools, as they go down the road to school renewal, should staff on the basis of purpose and priority, rather than convention, in regard to all existing roles.

3. These illustrations of governing models can be found in more detail in the organizational development work of Schmuck, Runkel, Arends, and Arends (1977), Glickman (1989), and Glickman and Allen (1992 and forthcoming).

Chapter 4

1. I am indebted to Emily Calhoun, who should receive much of the credit for the development of the data-source table. Her work on action research with schools has been most informative.

2. A caveat here is that the requirements of outside agencies for planning and data collection should be consistent with the school community's own priorities. If not, then the school may be forced to serve two masters and will need both a plan for complying with external mandates and a plan for its own school renewal. In Chapter Eight, I discuss district policies and parameters to avoid such a schism in local school operations.

3. This is why I prefer not to give workshops on school-based renewal to people in any one position (principals, teachers, and so on). I urge cross-representational groups to participate, so that all hear the same information, research, strategies, and concepts together. In this way, they can determine how to apply the work across the entire school community.

Chapter 5

1. In discussing money as an existing resource for schools, I am aware that there are schools and districts in America that are desperately underfunded for the challenges they face. Equalizing funding to schools is an issue that I mention only briefly in Chapters Eight, Nine, and Ten. Equi-

table funding is an issue that needs to be seriously addressed and corrected. Kozol (1992) addresses this issue head-on and is highly recommended reading.

2.   The sequence and phases of implementation were developed from the work of Bruce Joyce, Beverly Showers, Georgea Mohlman Langer, and Jane Stallings.

3.   Gene Hall and many of his associates have indicated at least six stages of concern that participants have with new ways of teaching and learning and corresponding levels of utilization. I have reduced their work to three stages.

Chapter 7

1.   Many of the ideas and questions in this section can be found in more depth in Schlechty (1990), Sizer (1984, 1992), Goodlad (1984), Oakes (1992), Darling-Hammond and Snyder (1992), and Glickman (1991).

2.   A particularly illuminating perspective on the failure of schools-within-schools can be found in McQuillan and Muncey (1992).

3.   I wrote about these dilemmas in Glickman (1990a).

Chapter 8

1.   For an excellent and highly readable essay on democracies developing from the inside out, I recommend Barber (1992).

2.   In most of my own work with schools, I set a level of at least 80 percent or more of faculty and staff approval by secret ballot, to ensure initial commitment to school renewal. The level could be adjusted according to local dictate. I realize that, in some settings, a 50 percent approval is close to miraculous.

Chapter 9

1.   I was introduced to the concept of legislated learning by Wise (1979), who prophesied at that time that the next decade would usher in more top-down regulation by author-

ities outside local schools. Wise also looked back and reflected on how accurate his prediction had been (Wise, 1988).

2. Barth (1990) has written cogently about these industries and the "list logic" (his term) that has been spawned. In this book, I have indicated my own list of dimensions, tasks, and elements. I do so as a way to convey my own understanding about school change, not to offer a prescription for others.

3. This scenario could just as well have been about a dysfunctional administrator.

Chapter 10

1. This story is borrowed from my friend Charles Wolfgang, who has narrated it in his writings and presentations.

2. Kozol (1992) should be a must-read for those who control the distribution of educational resources to schools at the district, state, and federal levels. That schools can be so unequal in resources is abhorrent in a society pledged to freedom and justice for all. In such extreme conditions, when students are doubled up in classrooms, chairs are unavailable, sewage leaks through the building, lighting is nonexistent, and unqualified substitutes are used as teachers, a school community may have to give first priority to nonteaching matters and scream for attention to physical conditions.

References

Barber, B. R. "Jihad vs. McWorld." *The Atlantic,* 1992, *265*(3), 53–65.

Barth, R. *Improving Schools from Within: Teachers, Parents, and Principals Can Make a Difference.* San Francisco: Jossey-Bass, 1990.

Boyer, E. L. *High School: A Report on Secondary Education in America.* New York: HarperCollins, 1983.

Bracey, G. W. "Why Can't They Be More Like Us?" *Phi Delta Kappan,* 1991, *73*(2), 105–117.

Bracey, G. W. "The Second Bracey Report on the Conditions of Public Education. *Phi Delta Kappan,* 1992, *74*(2), 104–117.

Brookover, W., Beady, C., Flood, P., Schweiter, J., and Wisenbaker, J. *School Social System and Students' Achievement: Schools Can Make a Difference.* New York: Praeger, 1979.

Chubb, J. E., and Moe, T. M. *Politics, markets, and America's schools.* Washington, D.C.: Brookings Institution, 1990.

Crow Dog, M., and Erdoes, R. *Lakota Woman.* New York: HarperCollins, 1990.

Darling-Hammond, L., and Snyder, J. "Reframing Accountability: Creating Learner-Centered Schools." In Lieberman (ed.), *The Changing Contexts of Teaching.* Chicago: University of Chicago Press, 1992.

Dewey, J. *Democracy and Education.* New York: Macmillan, 1916, pp. 86–87.

Dewey, J. "Presenting Thomas Jefferson." *Later Works,* no. 14 (202), 1940, pp. 213–218.

Elam, S. M., Rose, L. C., and Gallup, A. M. "The 24th Annual Gallup/Phi Delta Kappa Poll of the Public's Attitudes Towards the Public School." *Phi Delta Kappan,* 1992, *74*(1), 41–53.

"Foxfire Core Practices." *Hands On,* 1991, *40,* 4–5.

Fullan, M. G., and Miles, M. B. "Getting Reform Right: What Works and What Doesn't." *Phi Delta Kappan,* 1992, *73*(10), 745–752.

Glickman, C. D. *Shared Governance at Oglethorpe County High School.* Athens, Ga.: Monographs in Education, 1989.

Glickman, C. D. "Pushing School Reform to a New Edge: The Seven Ironies of Empowerment." *Phi Delta Kappan,* 1990a, *72*(1), 68–75.

Glickman, C. D. *Supervision of Instruction: A Developmental Approach.* (2nd ed.) Boston, Mass.: Allyn and Bacon, 1990b.

Glickman, C. D. "Pretending Not to Know What We Know." *Educational Leadership,* 1991, *48*(8), 4–10.

Glickman, C. D., and Allen, L. *The League of Professional Schools: Lessons from the Field.* Vol. 1. Athens: Program for School Improvement, University of Georgia, 1992.

Glickman, C. D., and Allen, L. *The League of Professional Schools: Lessons from the Field.* Vol. 2. Athens: Program for School Improvement, University of Georgia, forthcoming.

Glickman, C. D., Allen, L., and Lunsford, B. "Facilitation of Internal Change." Paper presented to the annual meeting of the American Educational Research Association, San Francisco, 1992.

Goodlad, J. I. *A Place Called School: Prospects for the Future.* New York: McGraw-Hill, 1984.

Graham, P. A. *S.O.S.: Sustain Our Schools.* New York: Hill and Wang, 1992.

Grimmett, P. P., Rostad, O. P., and Ford, B. "The Transformation of Supervision." In C. D. Glickman (ed.), *Supervision in Transition.* Alexandria, Va.: Association for Supervision and Curriculum Development, 1992.

Guttmann, A. *Democratic Education.* Princeton, N.J.: Princeton University Press, 1987.

Havel, V. "The Velvet Hangover." *Harpers,* 1990, *281*(1685), 18–21.

"If Everyone Eligible Voted, Who Would Win?" *St. Albans Messenger,* 1992, *130*(451), 1–14.

Jaeger, R. M. "World-Class Standards, Choice, and Privatization: Weak Measurement Serving Presumptive Policy." *Phi Delta Kappan,* 1992, *74*(2), 118–128.

Kozol, J. *Savage Inequalities: Children in America's Schools.* New York: HarperCollins, 1992.

Little, J. W. "Norms of Collegiality and Experimentation: Workplace Conditions of School Success." *American Educational Research Journal,* 1982, *19*(3), 325–340.

McNeil, L. N. "Contradictions of Control. Part 2: Teachers, Students, and Curriculum." *Phi Delta Kappan,* 1988, *69*(6), 432–438.

McQuillan, P. J., and Muncey, D. E. "School-Within-a-School Restructuring and Faculty Divisiveness." Unpublished paper, School Ethnography Project, Brown University, 1992.

Oakes, J. "Can Tracking Research Inform Practice?" *Educational Researcher,* 1992, *21*(4), 12–20.

Padover, S. K. *Democracy.* Westport, Conn.: Greenwood, 1939. (Reprinted in 1970).

Rosenholtz, S. *Teachers' Workplace: The Social Organization of Schools.* New York: Longman, 1989.

Rutter, M., Maughan, B., Mortimore, P., Ouston, J., and Smith, A. *Fifteen Thousand Hours: Secondary Schools and Their Effects on Children.* Cambridge, Mass.: Harvard University Press, 1979.

Schlechty, P. *Schools for the 21st Century: Leadership Imperatives for Educational Reform.* San Francisco: Jossey-Bass, 1990.

Schmuck, R. A., Runkel, P., Arends, J. H., and Arends, R. I. *The Second Handbook of Organizational Development in Schools.* Palo Alto, Calif.: Mayfield, 1977.

Sizer, T. *Horace's Compromise: The Dilemma of the American High School.* Boston: Houghton Mifflin, 1984.

Sizer, T. *Horace's School: Redesigning the American High School.* Boston: Houghton Mifflin, 1992.

Teaching and Learning Task Force. "Report on Learning." Unpublished manuscript, Georgia Partnership for Excellence in Education, 1991.

Westbrook, R. B. *John Dewey and American Democracy.* Ithaca, N.Y.: Cornell University Press, 1991.

Wise, A. *Legislated Learning.* Berkeley: University of California Press, 1979.

Wise, A. "The Two Conflicting Trends in School Reform." *Phi Delta Kappan,* 1988, *69*(5), 328–333.

Wilson, D. L. "Thomas Jefferson and the Character Issue." *Atlantic,* 1992, *270*(5), 57–74.

Index

A

Ability grouping, 94
Action: and planning, 80; and study, 54–57
Action research, 50–51
Allen, L., 100, 174 n1, 175 n3, ch3
American Educational Research Association, 58–59
Arends, J. H., 175 n3, ch3
Arends, R. I., 175 n3, ch3
Assessment, student, 72–73
Authoritarian and advisory approach, 83–84, 85, 87
Authorities, external: dependence on, 141–142; and reform of schools, 152
Autonomy, 93–94; and educational practices, 94–97; increasing, 122–123; and successful schools, 17

B

Barber, B. R., 151, 176 n1, ch8
Barth, R., 174 n1, ch2, 177 n2, ch9
Beady, C., 16
Boyer, E. L., 20
Bracey, G. W., 3
Brookover, W., 16
Bruner, J., 132
Budget, instructional, 73–74

C

Calhoun, E., 175 n1, ch4
Change: approaches to, 83–85; conflict about, 92–93; and disequilibrium, 82–83; schoolwide, 99–100; sequence, emphasis, and pace of, 142–144. *See also* Educational change
Charter, 29, 46–47, 67; approval percentage in, 45–46; and democracy in schools, 41–44; Peakview Schools, 165–167; sample, 159–164. *See also* Governance
Children, current condition of, 4–5
Choice, and approach to change, 85
Choice-and-voucher movement, 11–12, 173 n3
Chubb, J. E., 17
Citizenship, and goal, 8
Classrooms, 96
Coaching, 70–71, 92
Collaborative approach, 84, 85, 87
Collegial schools, 17–18, 22–23
Communication: and controversy, 105; faculty access to, 20–21
Community, and public school change, 103–106, 151–152
Competition, interschool, 100–102
Comprehensive-impact decisions, 33, 34
Concern: developmental level of, 87; stages of, 76–79

183